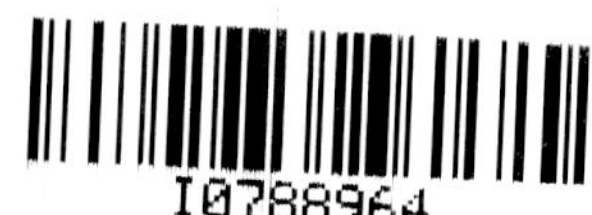

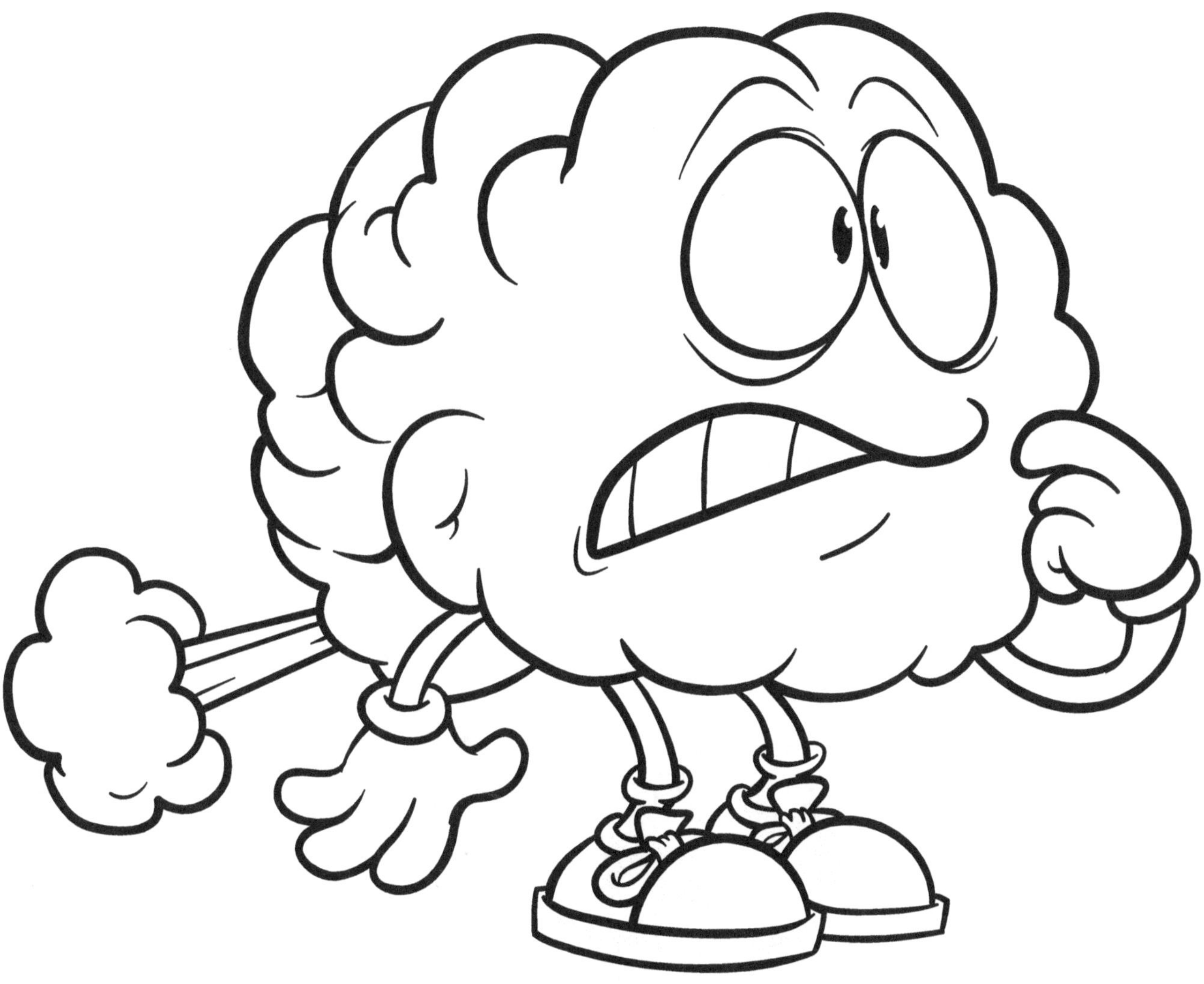

# THIS BOOK BELONGS TO

_______________________________

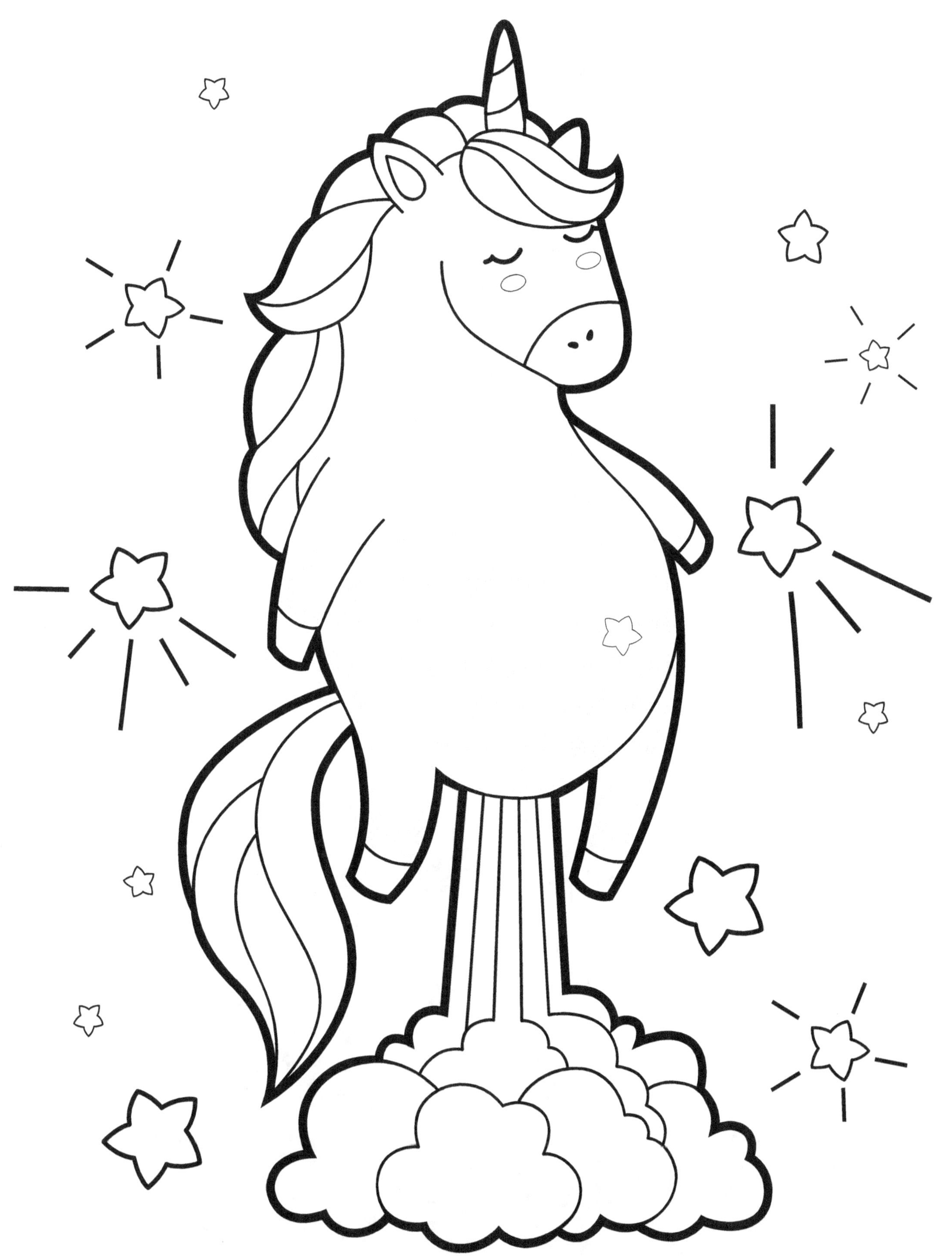

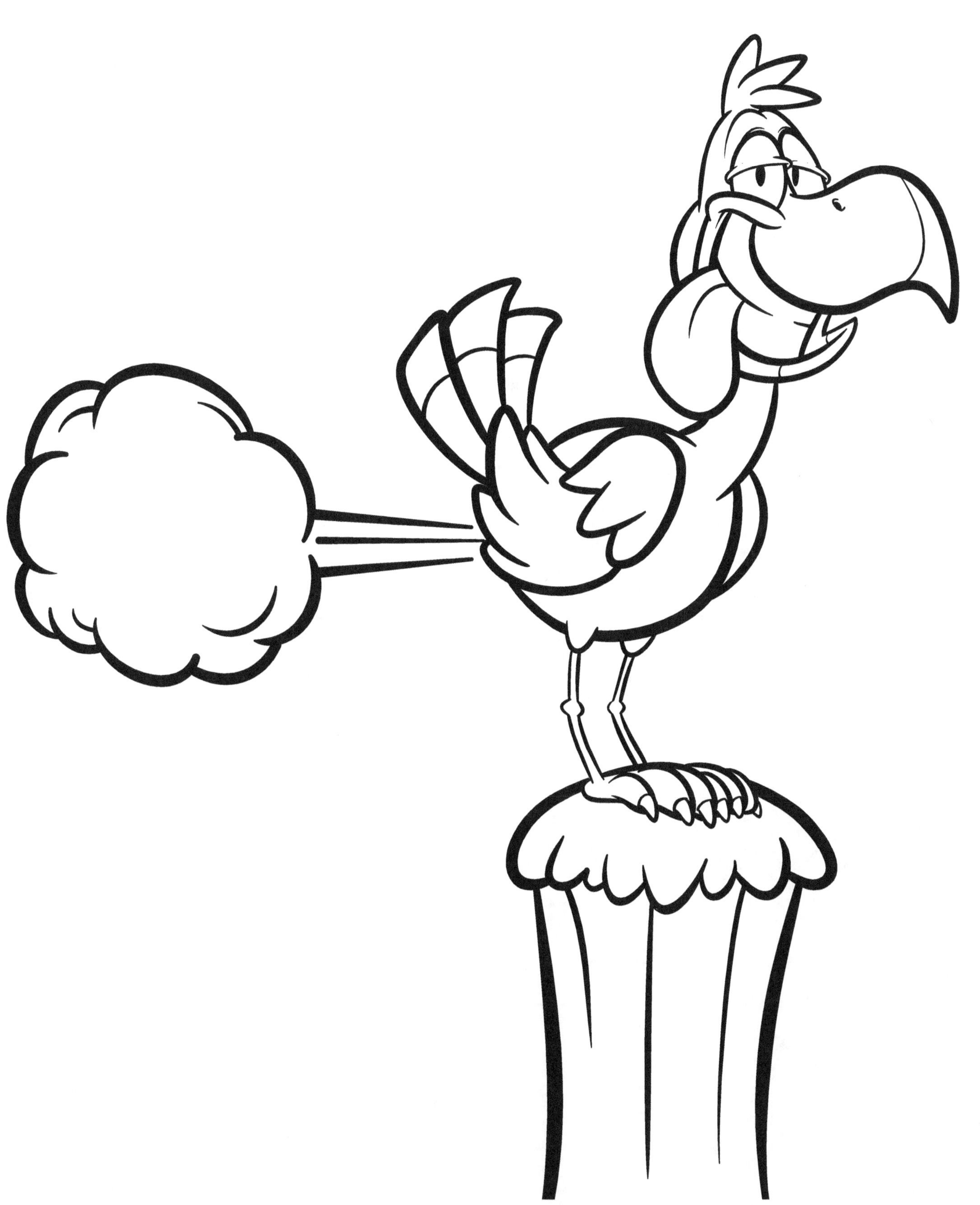

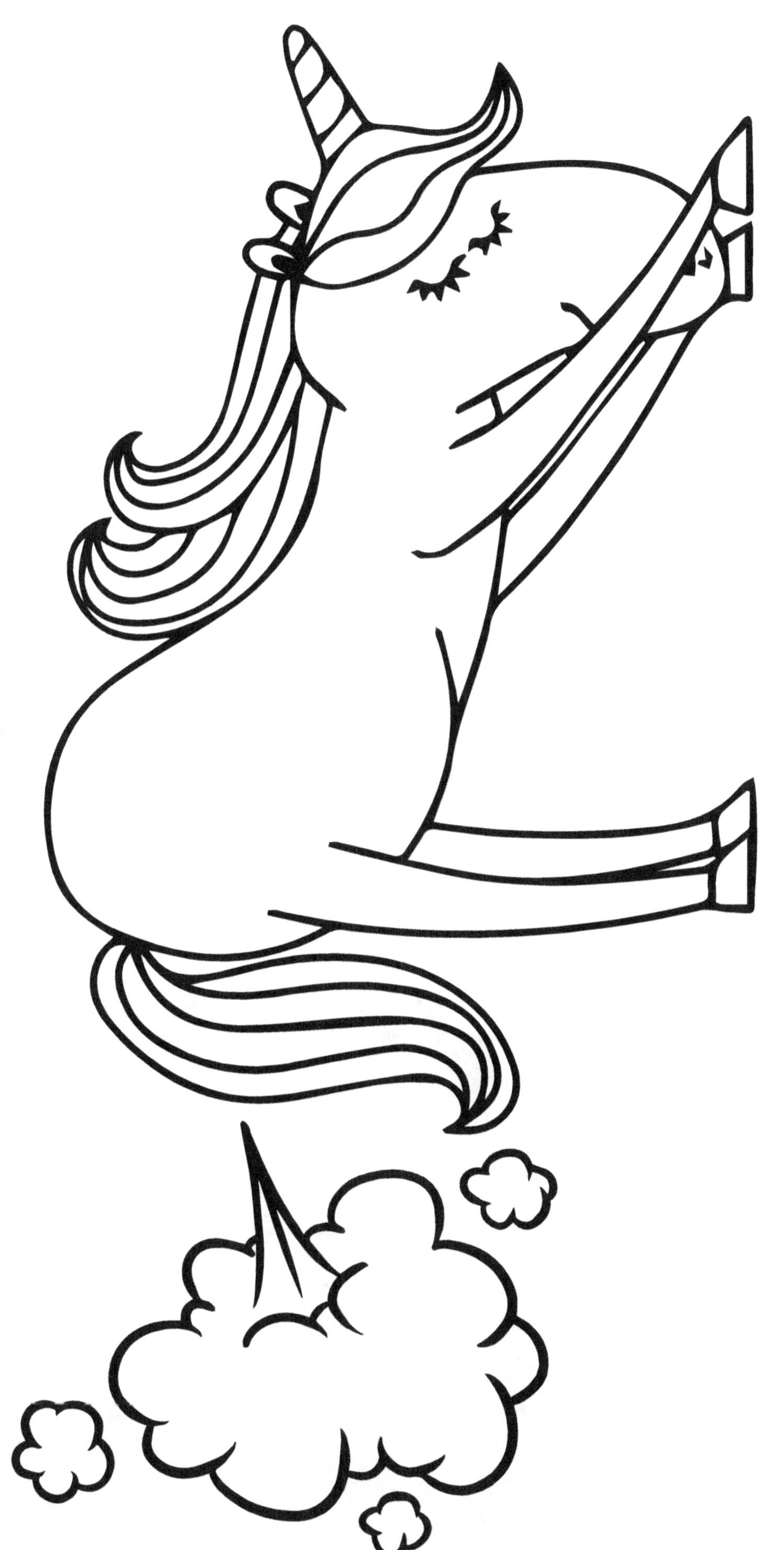

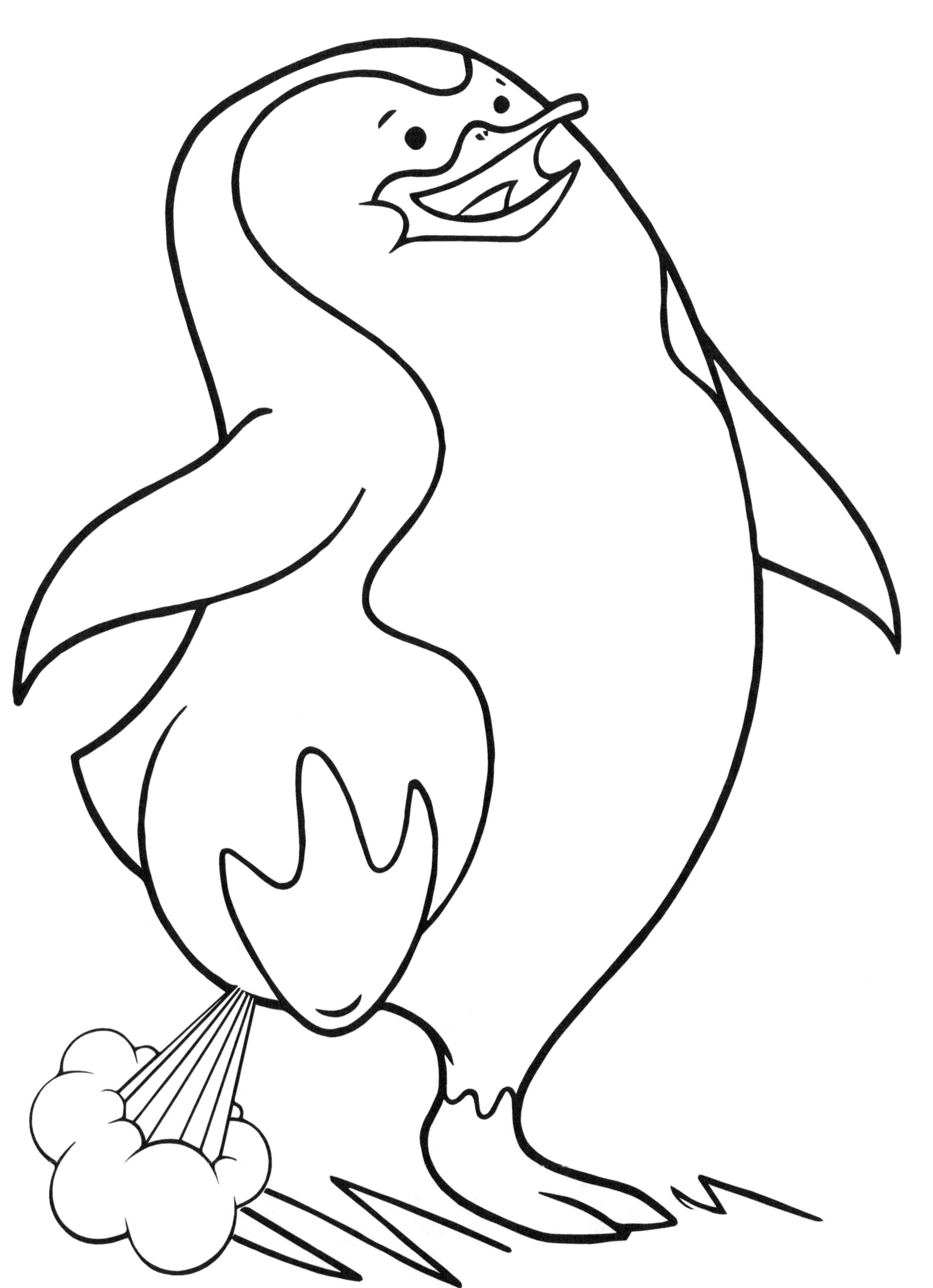

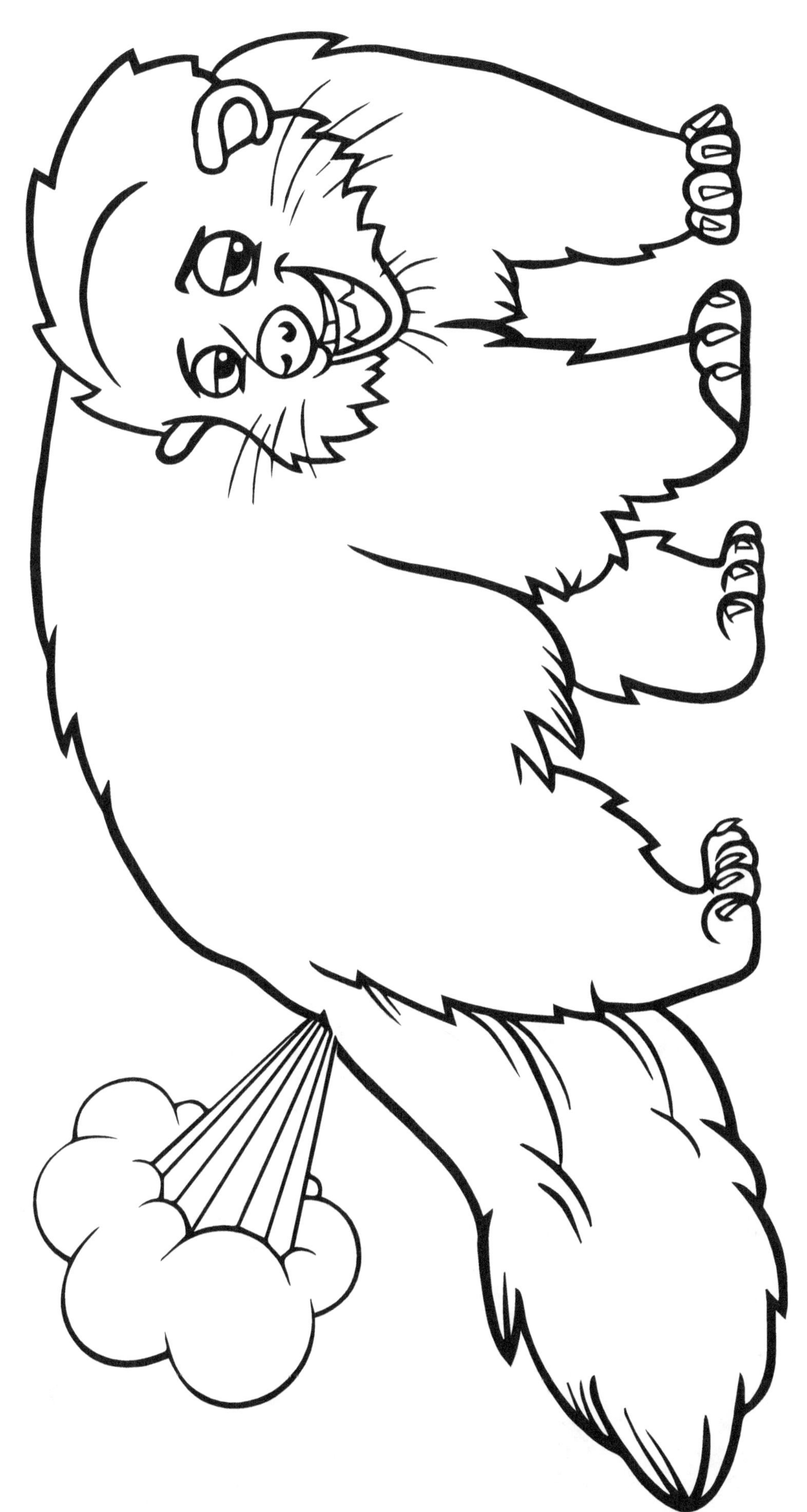

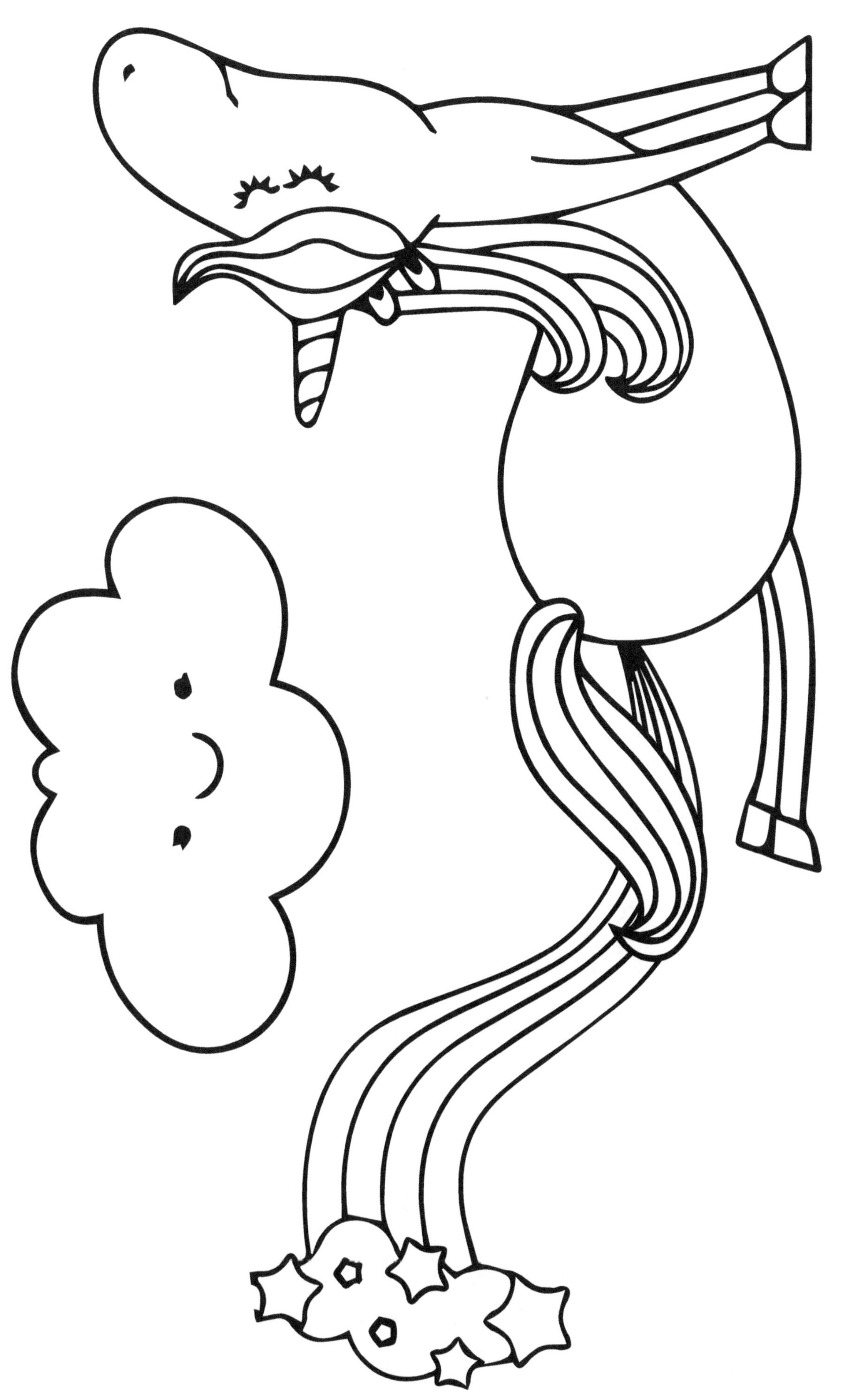

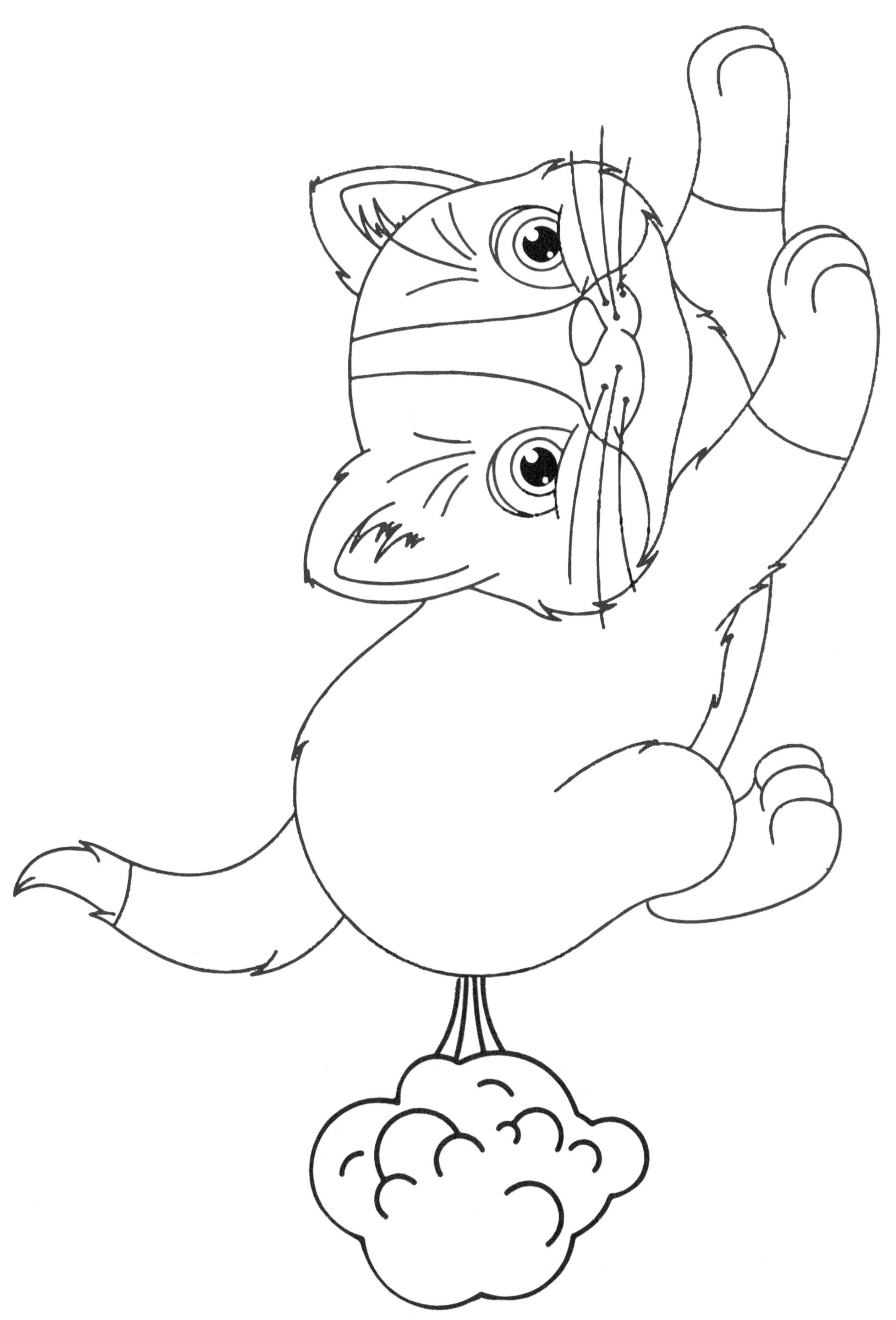

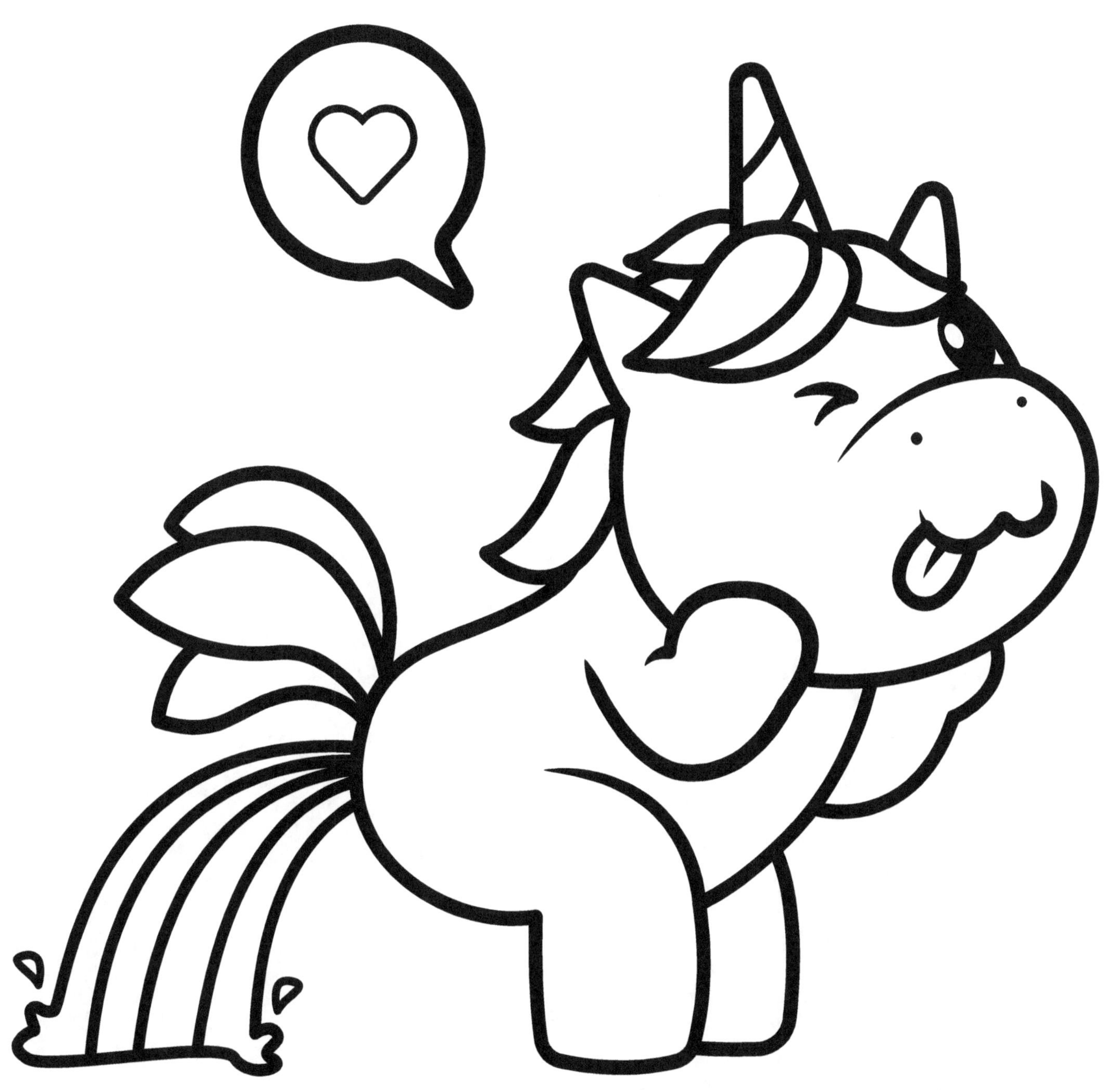

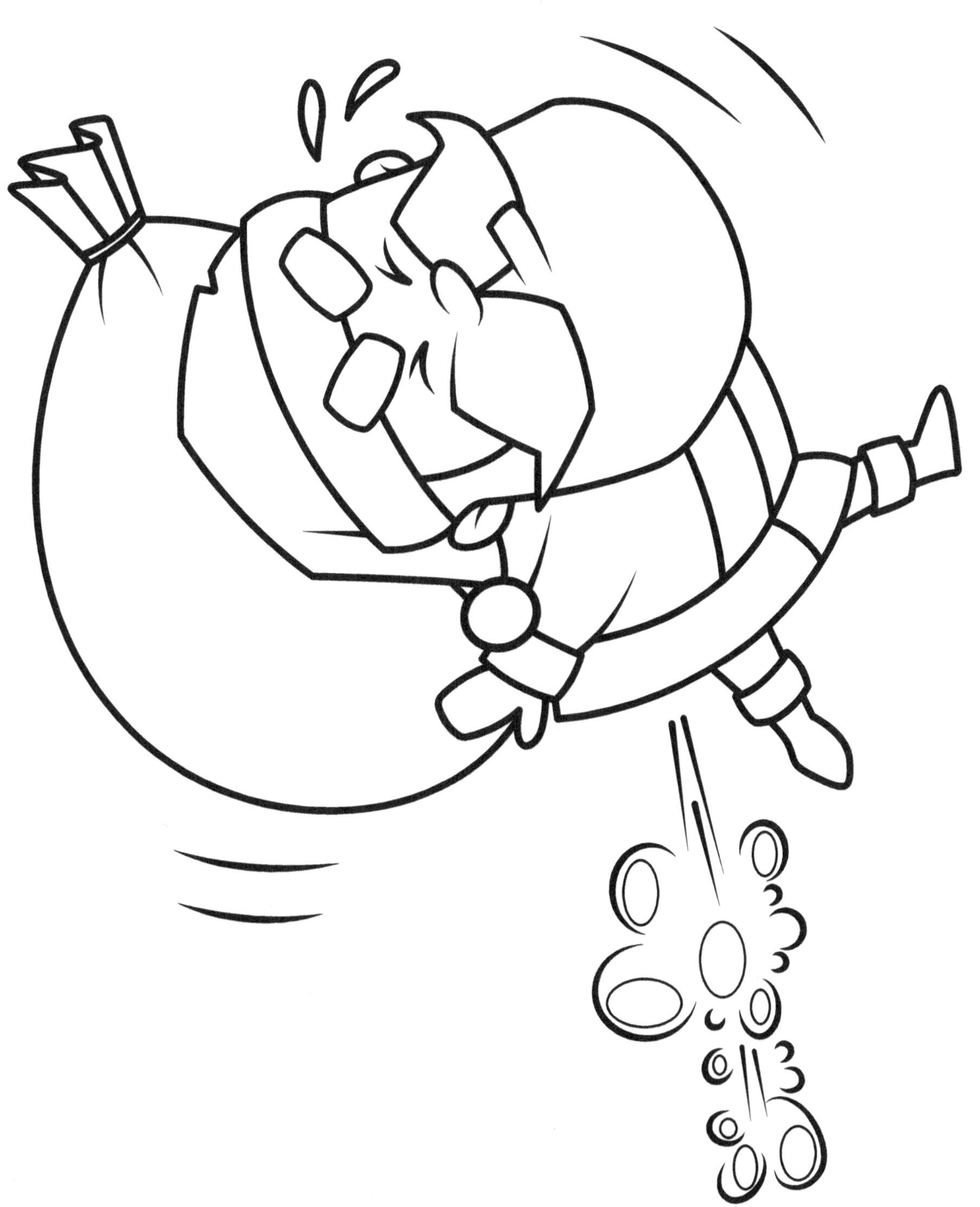

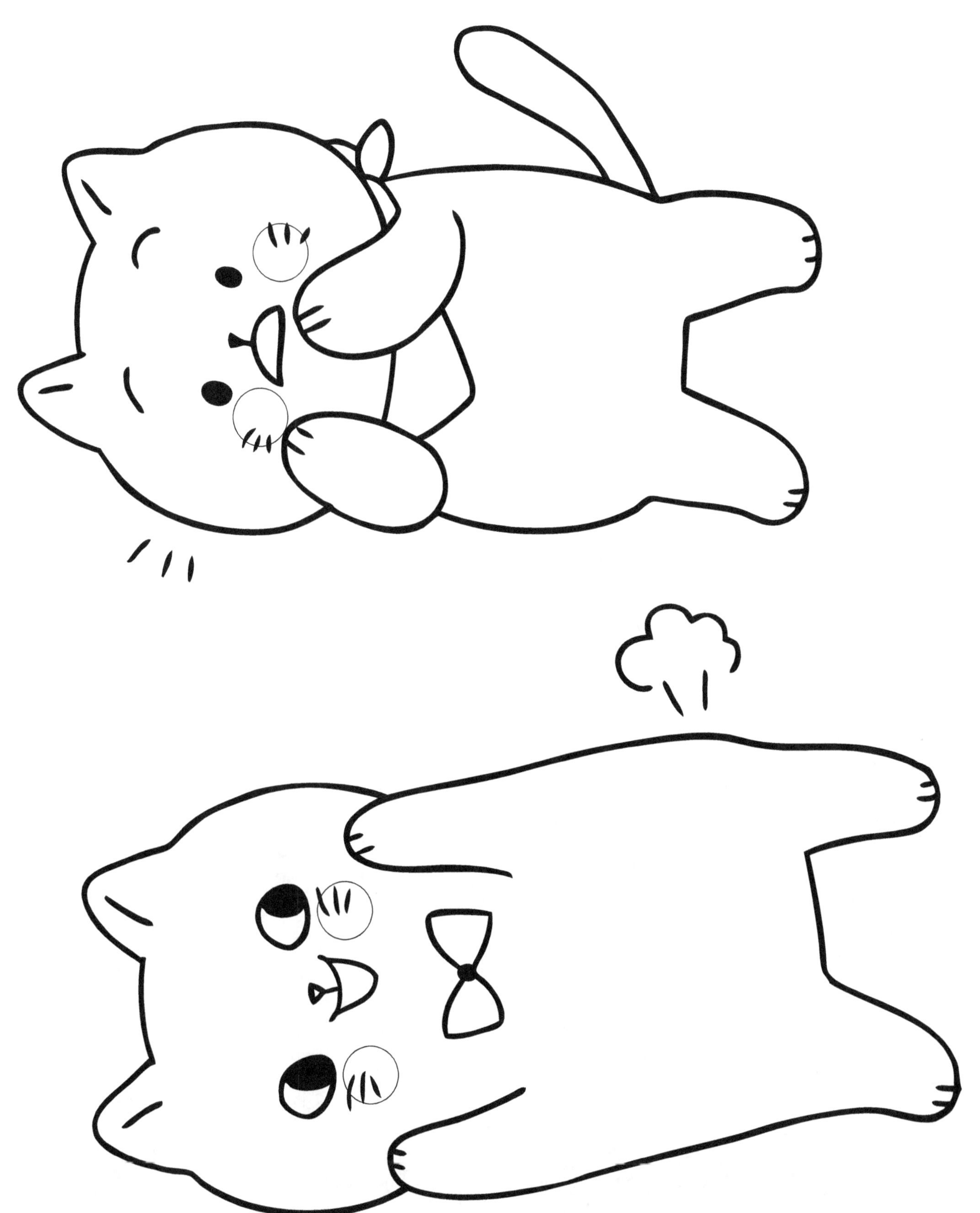

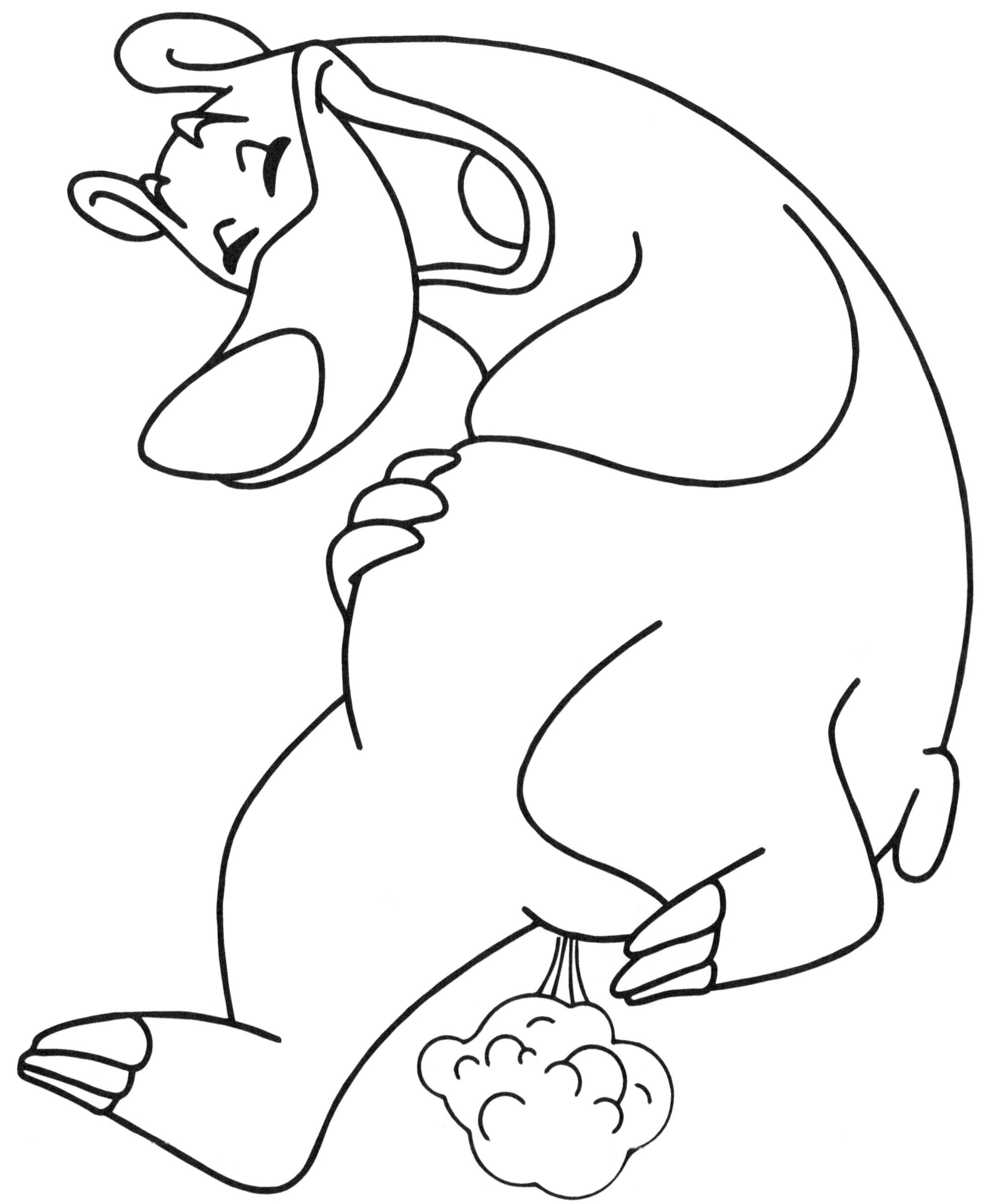

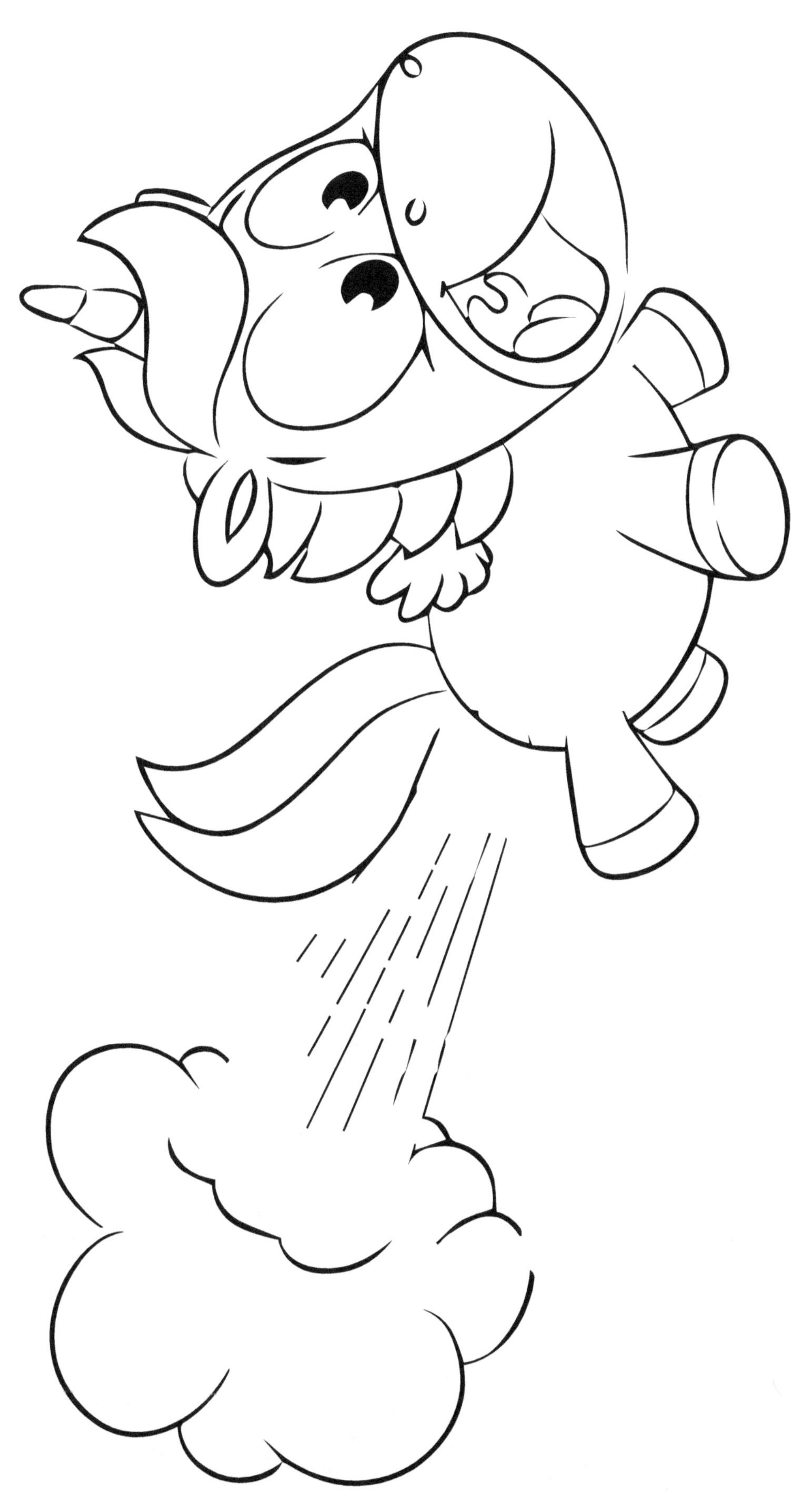

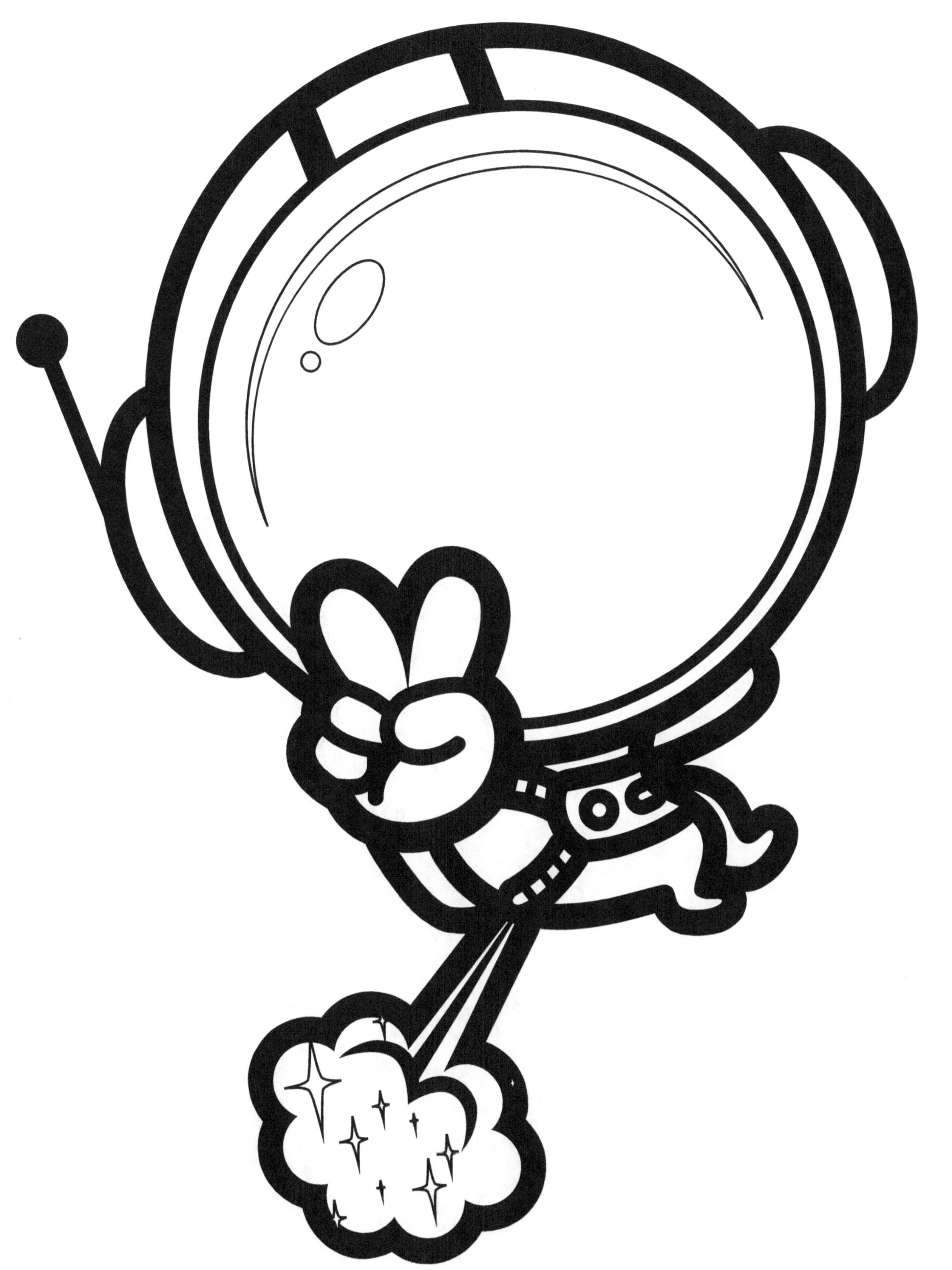

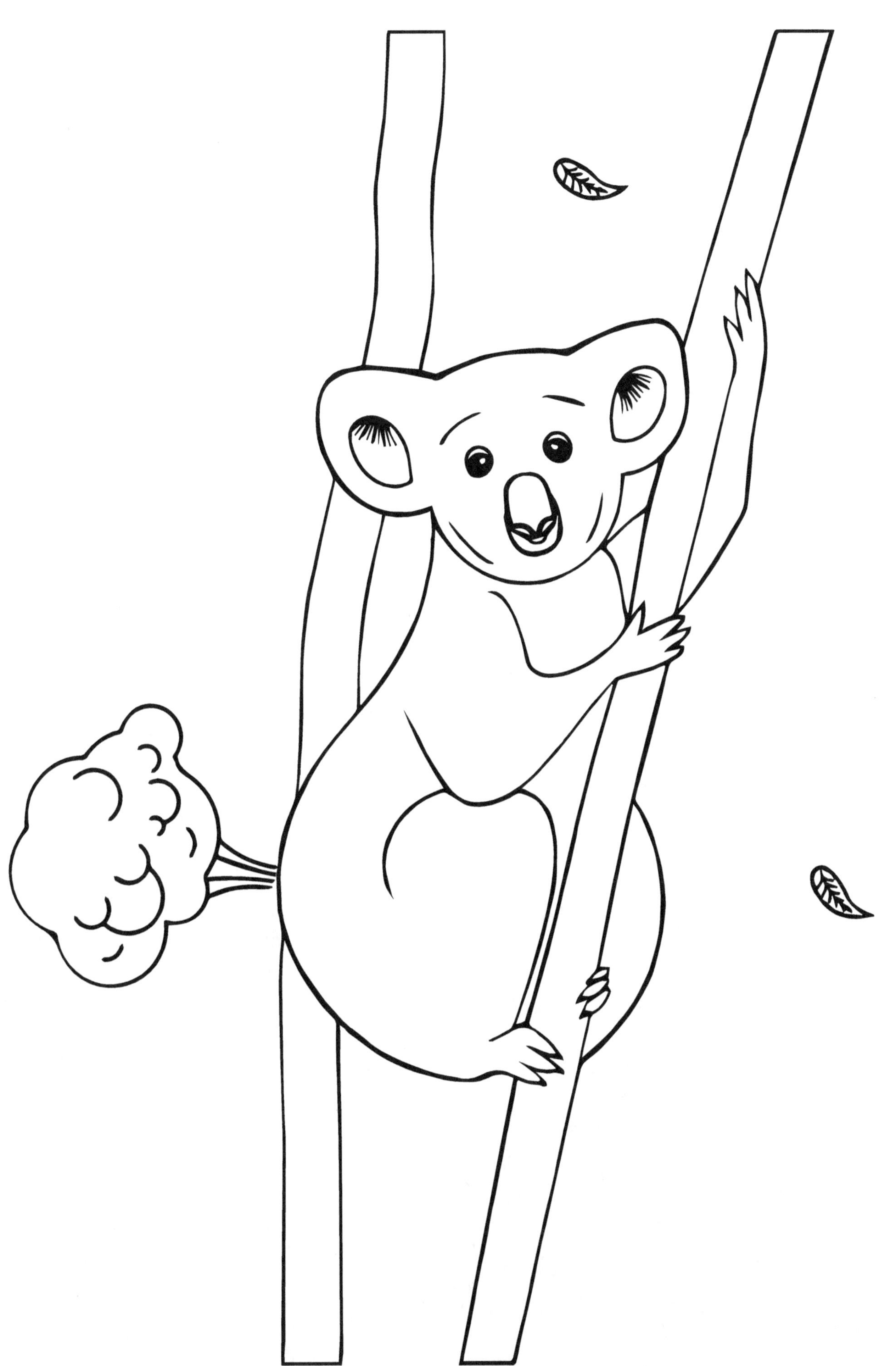

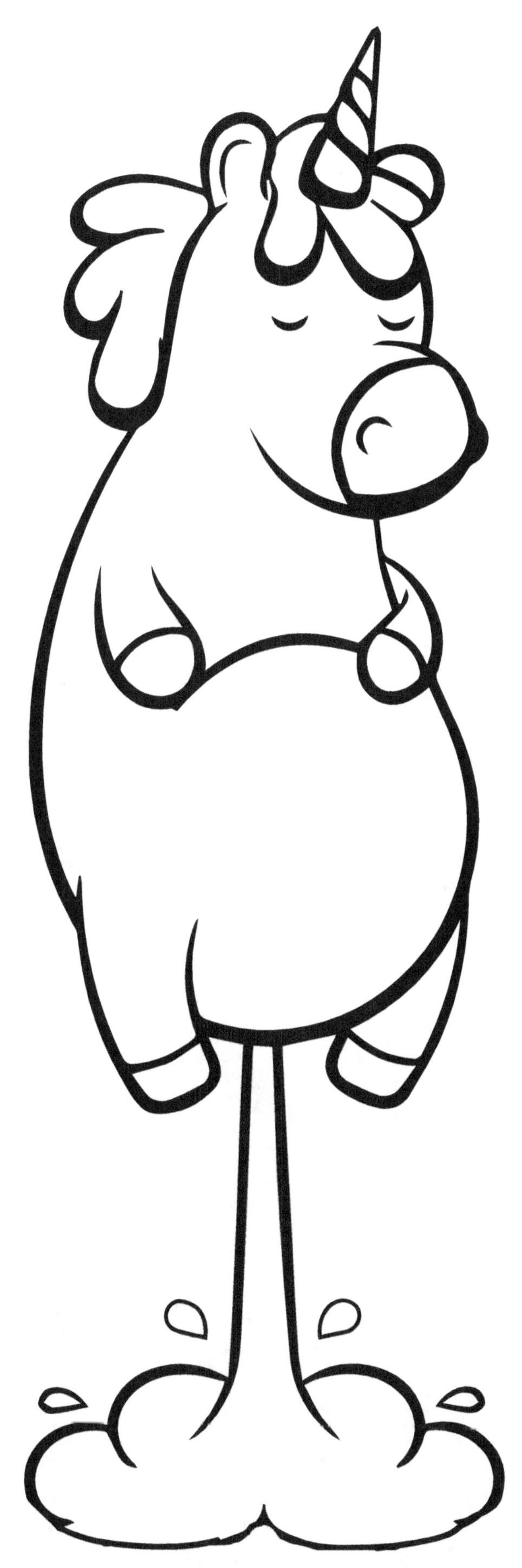

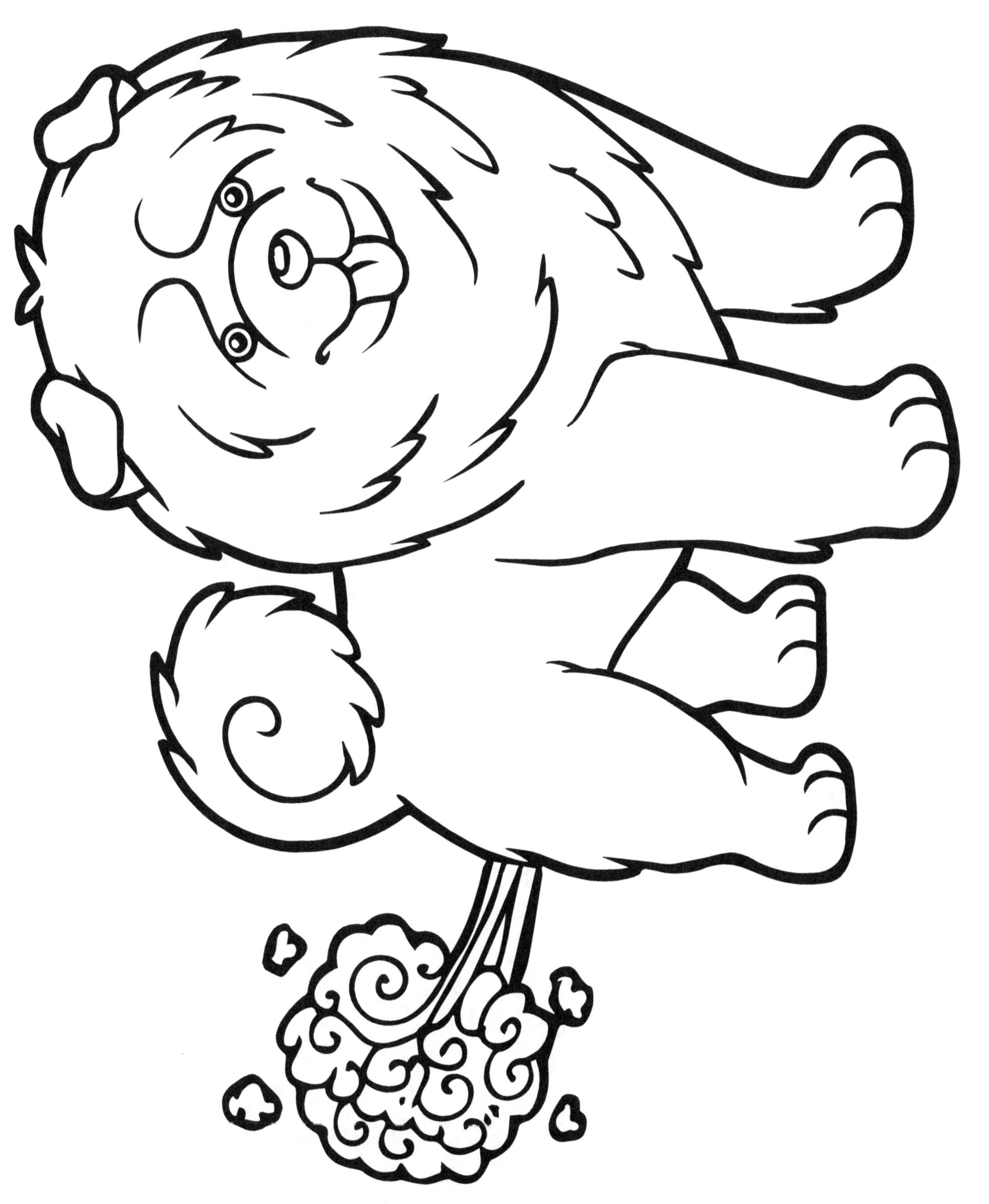

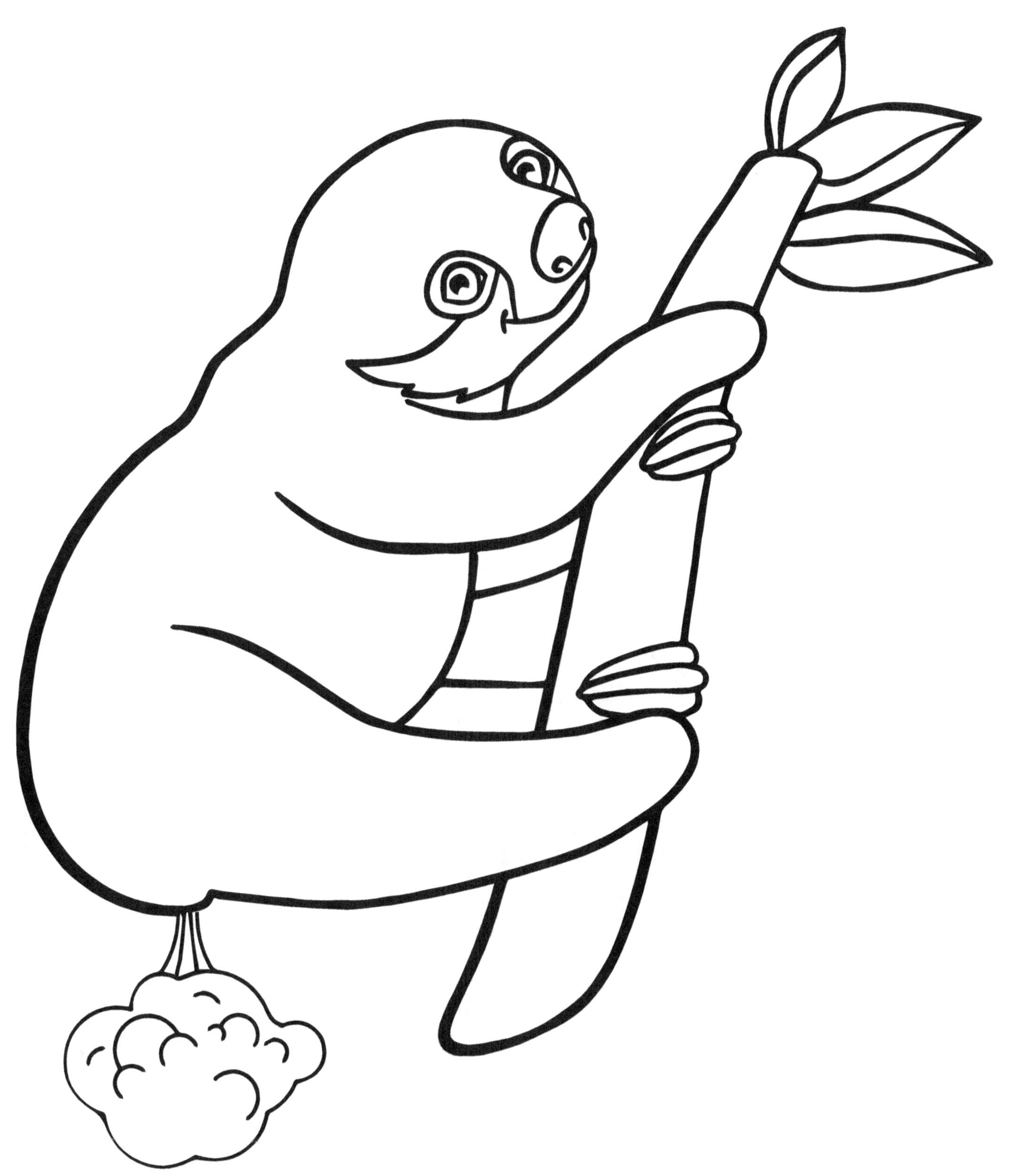

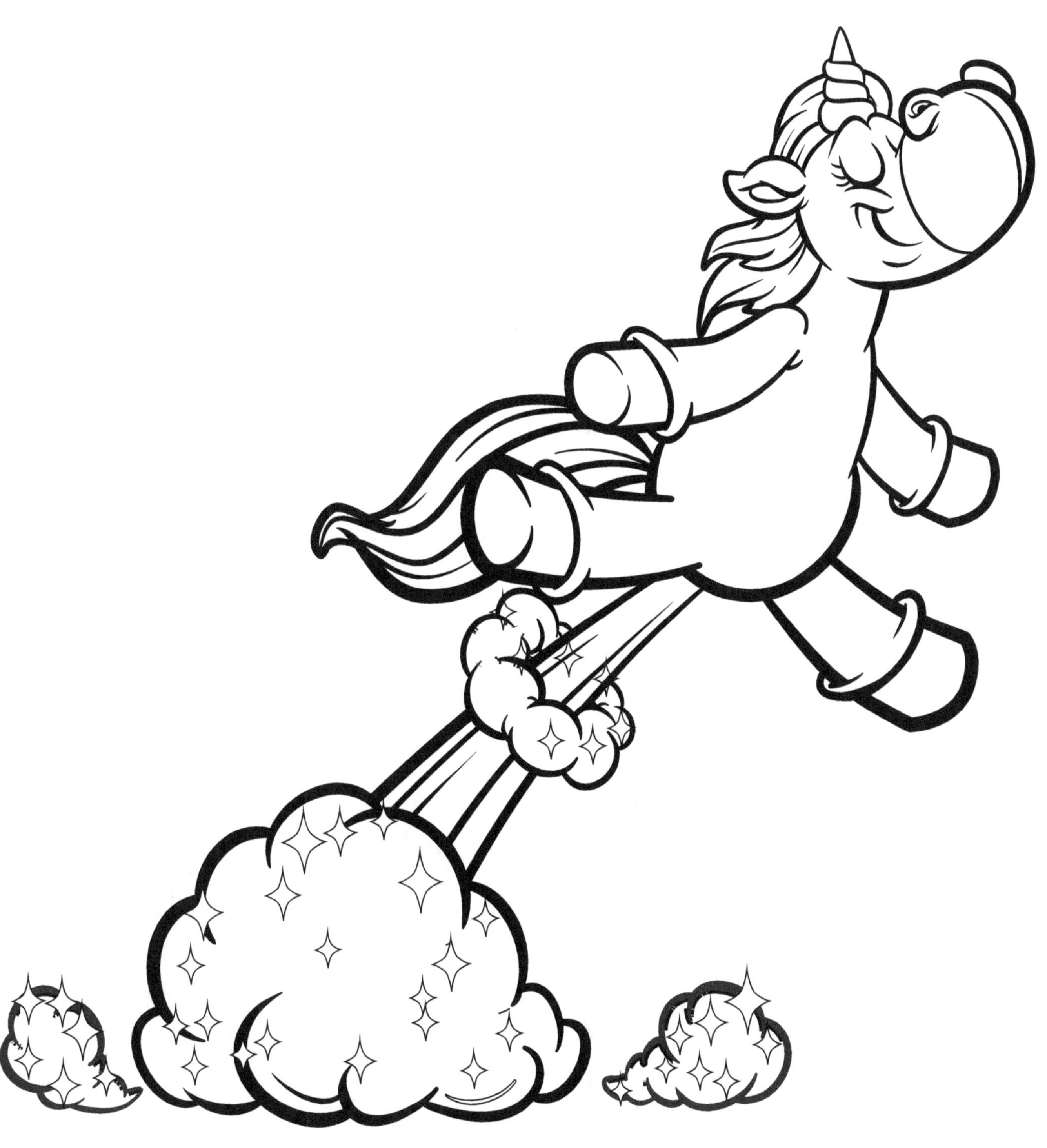

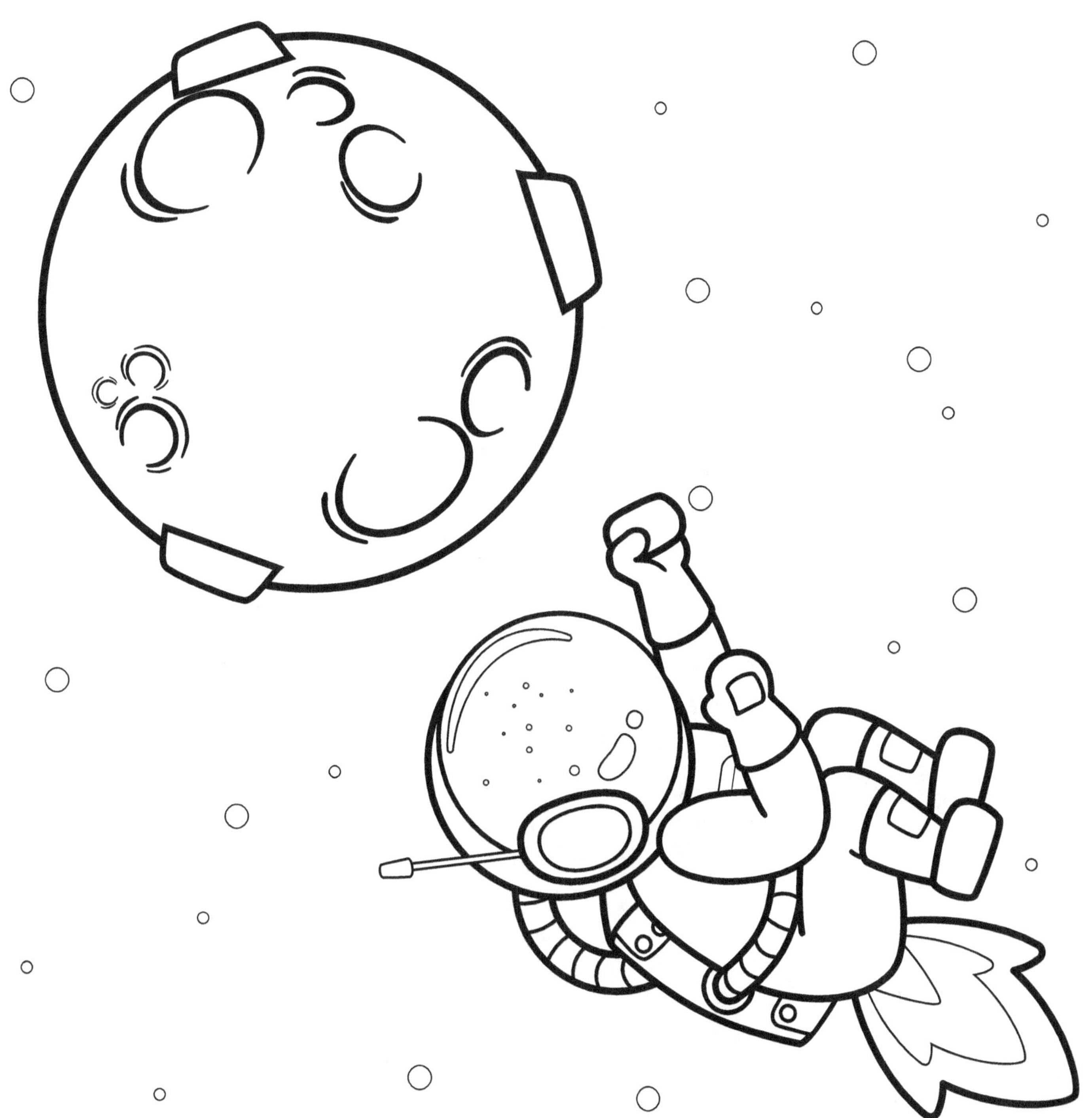

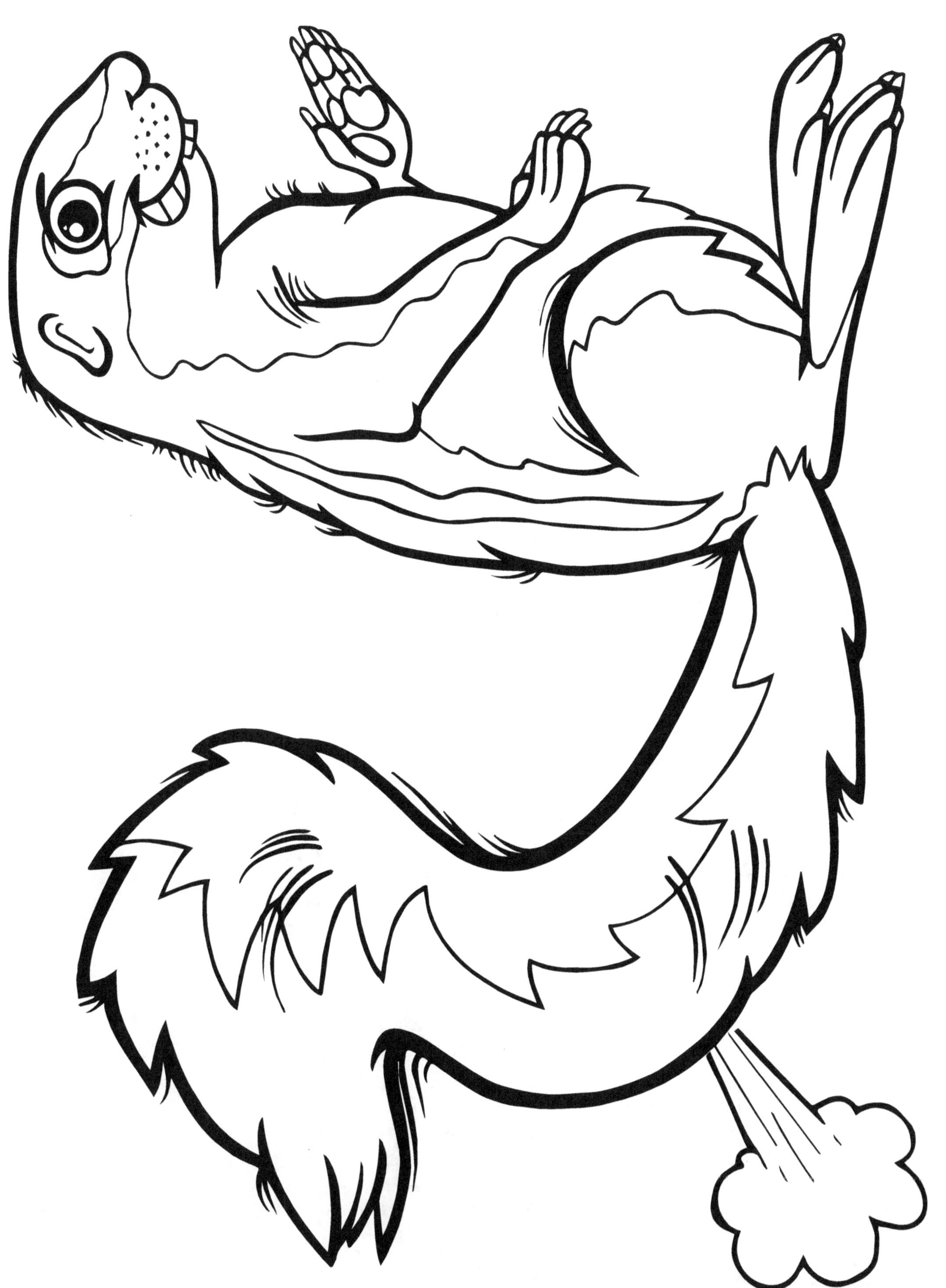

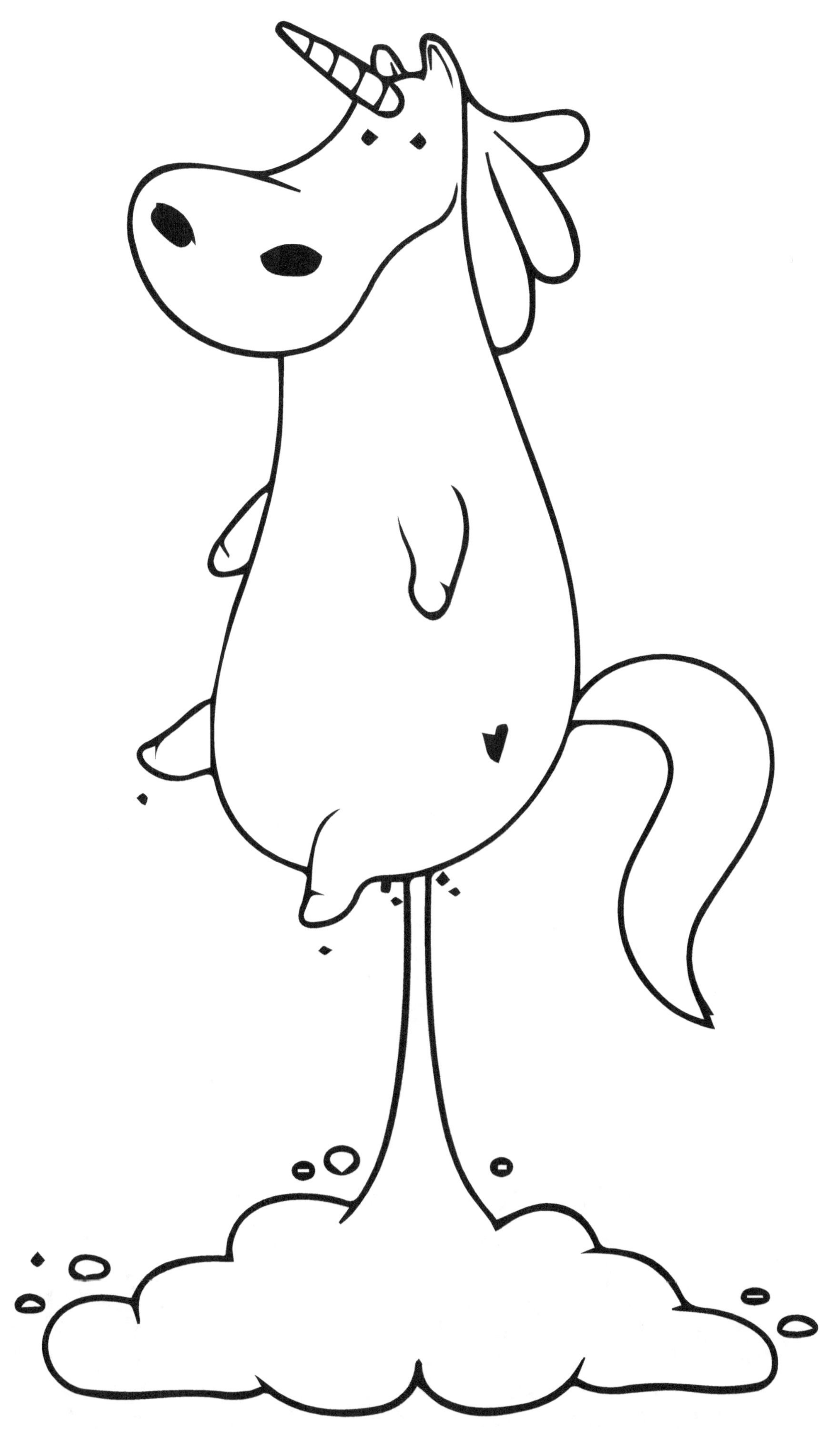

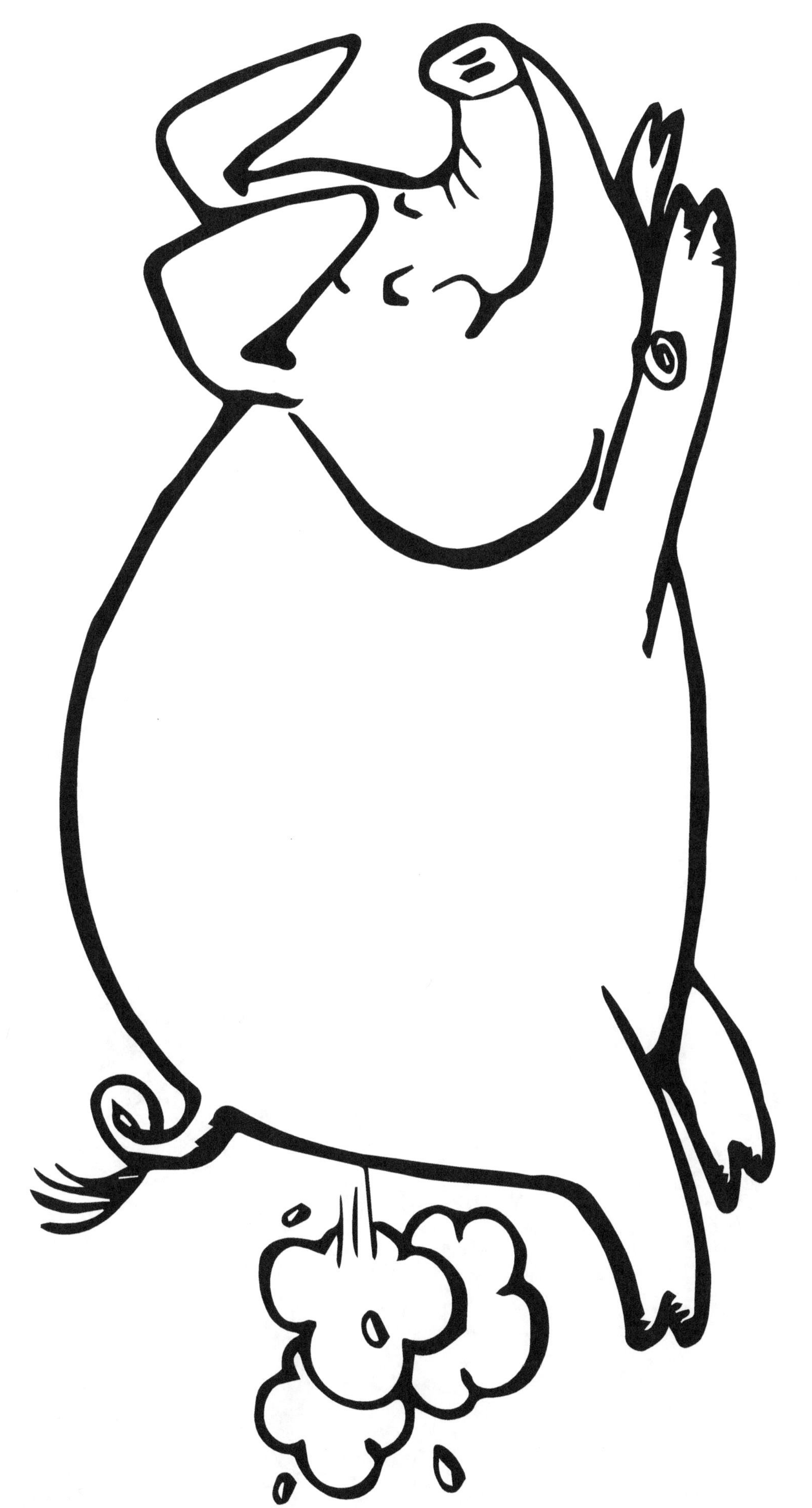

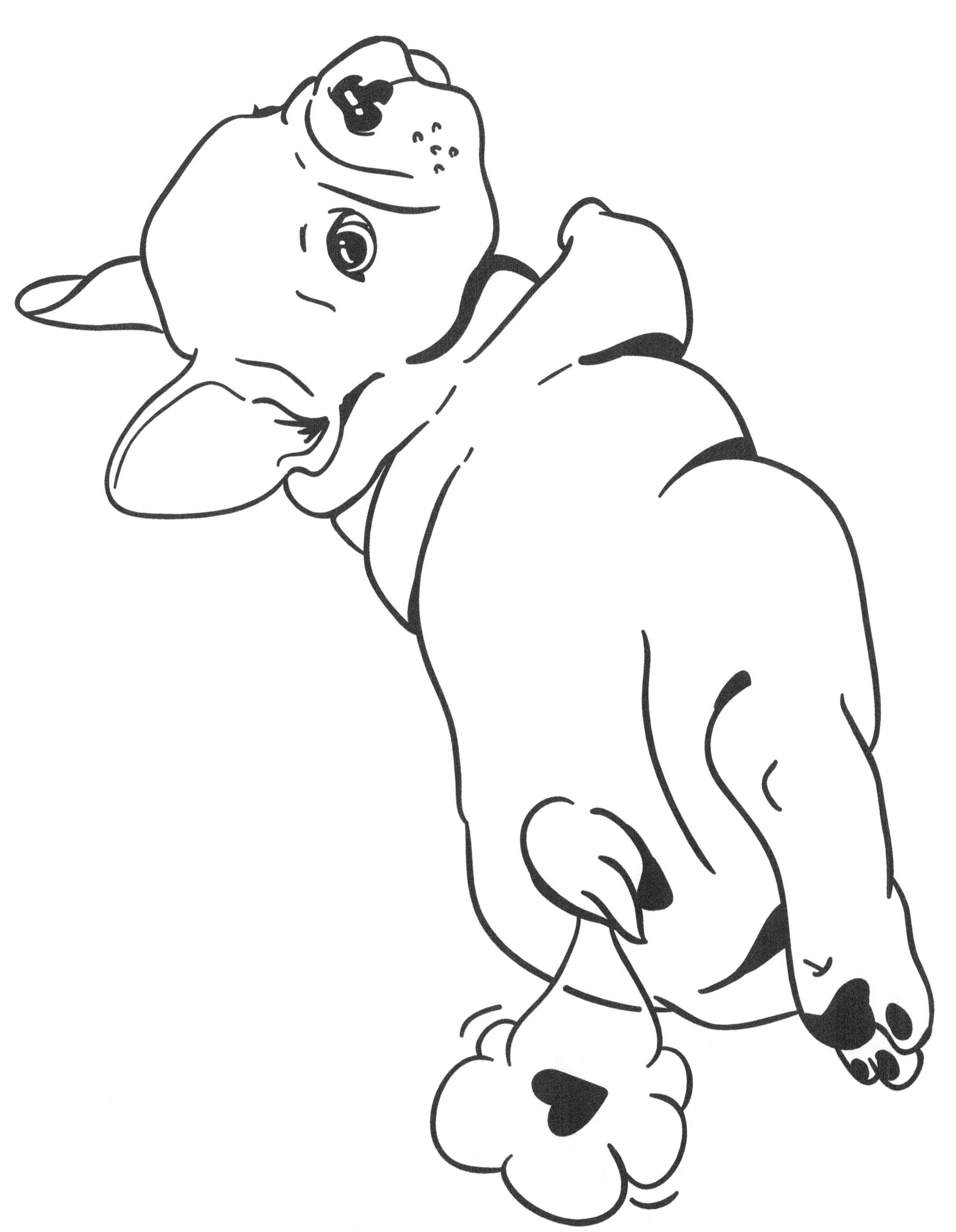

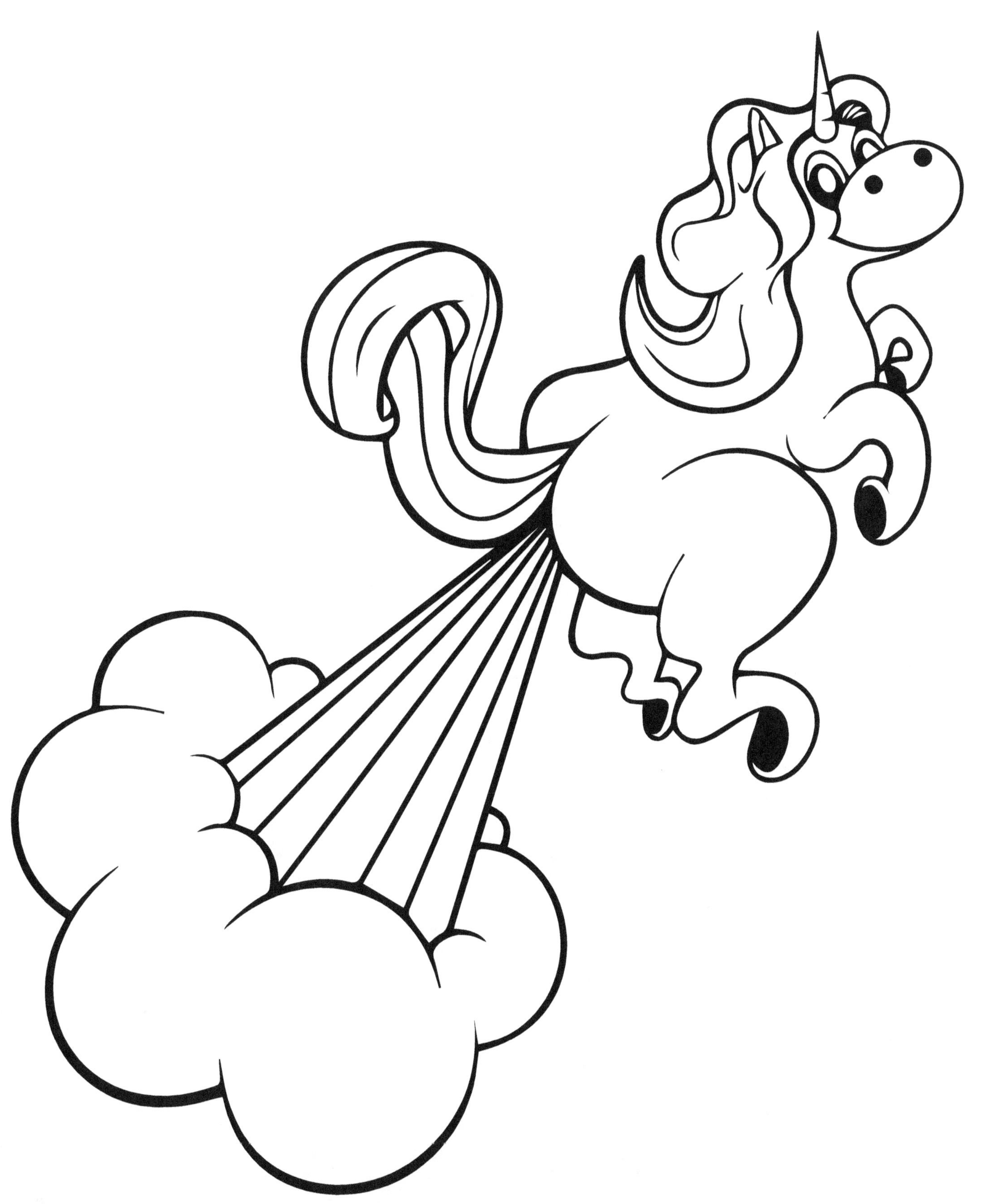

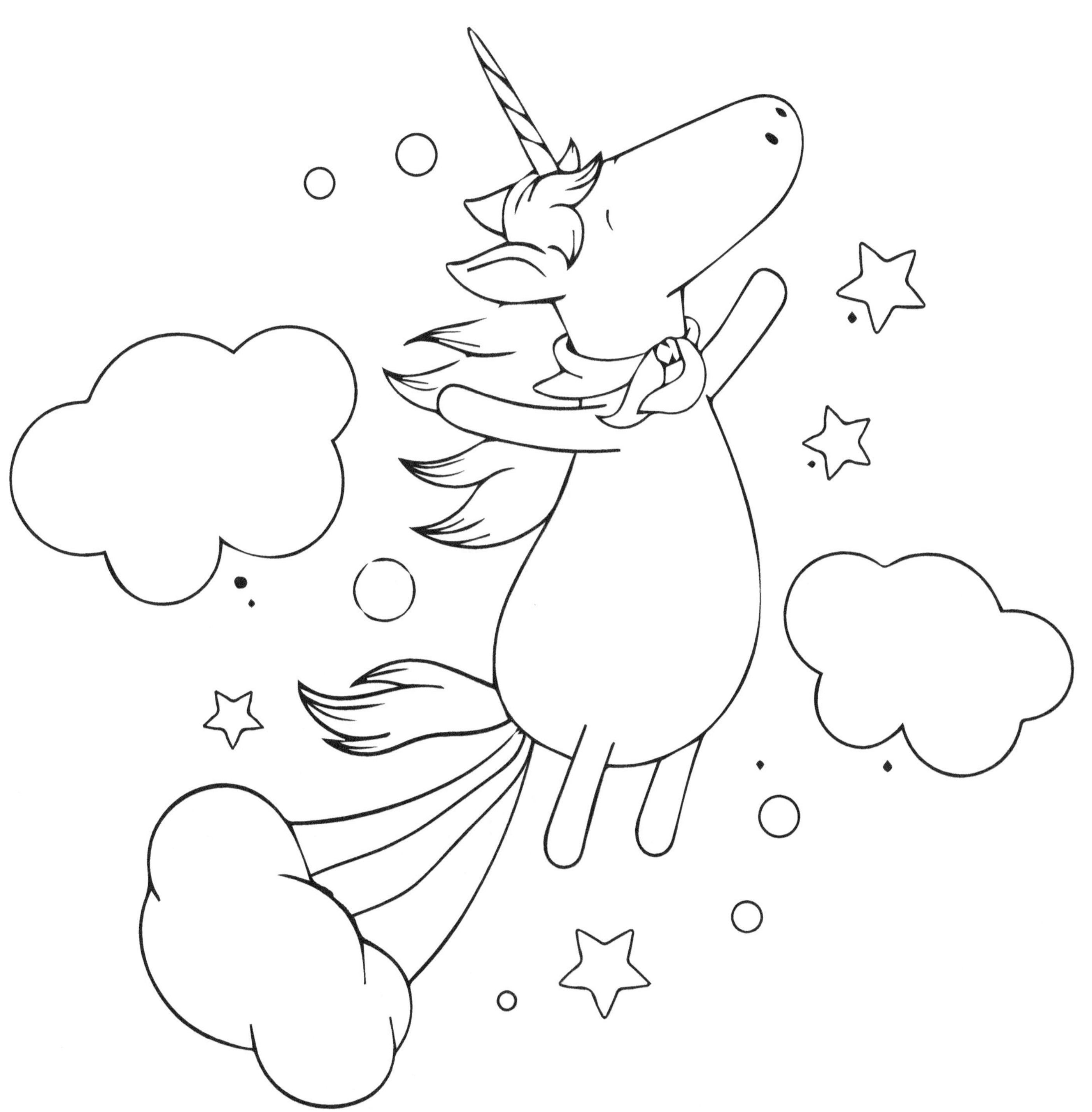

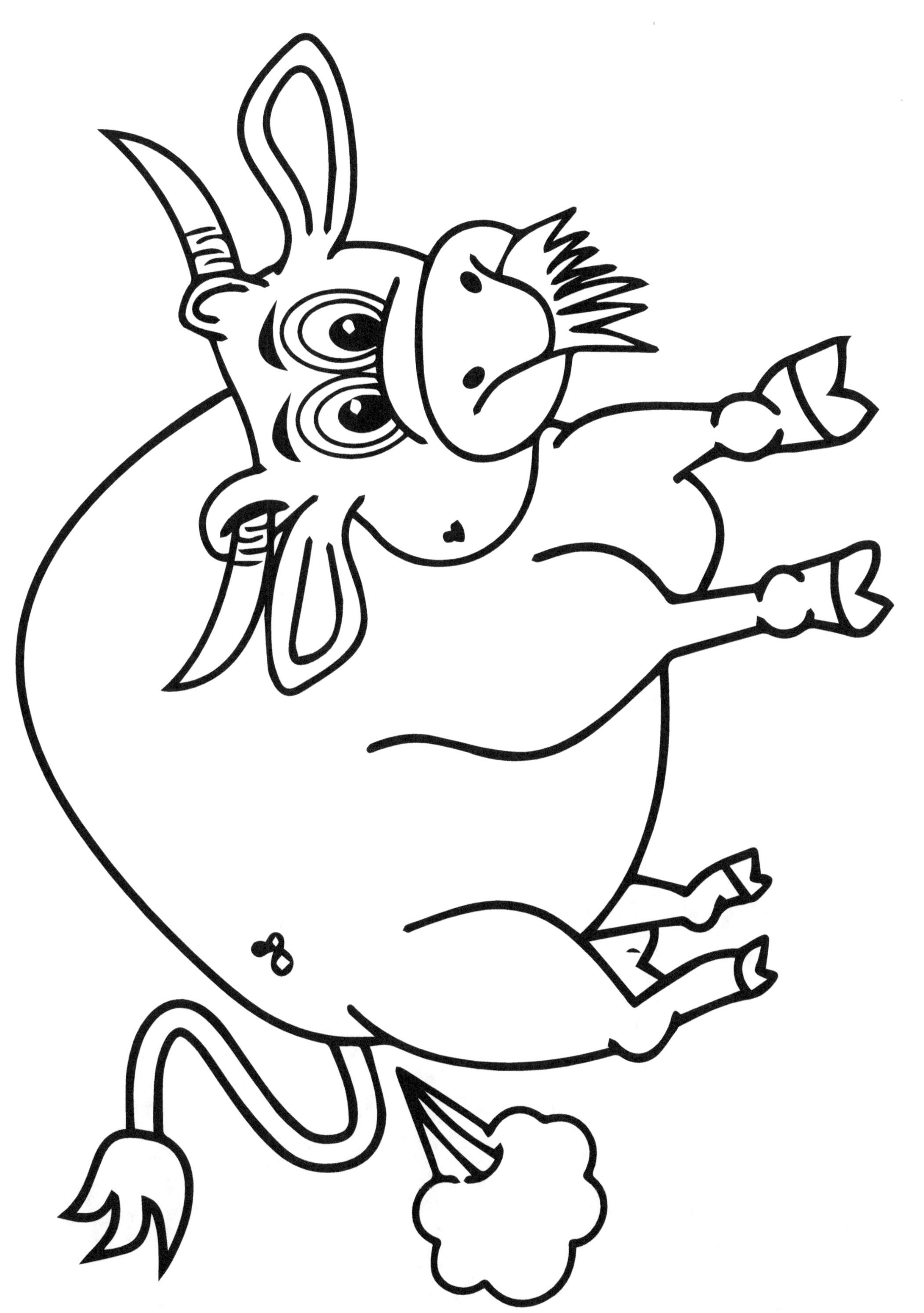

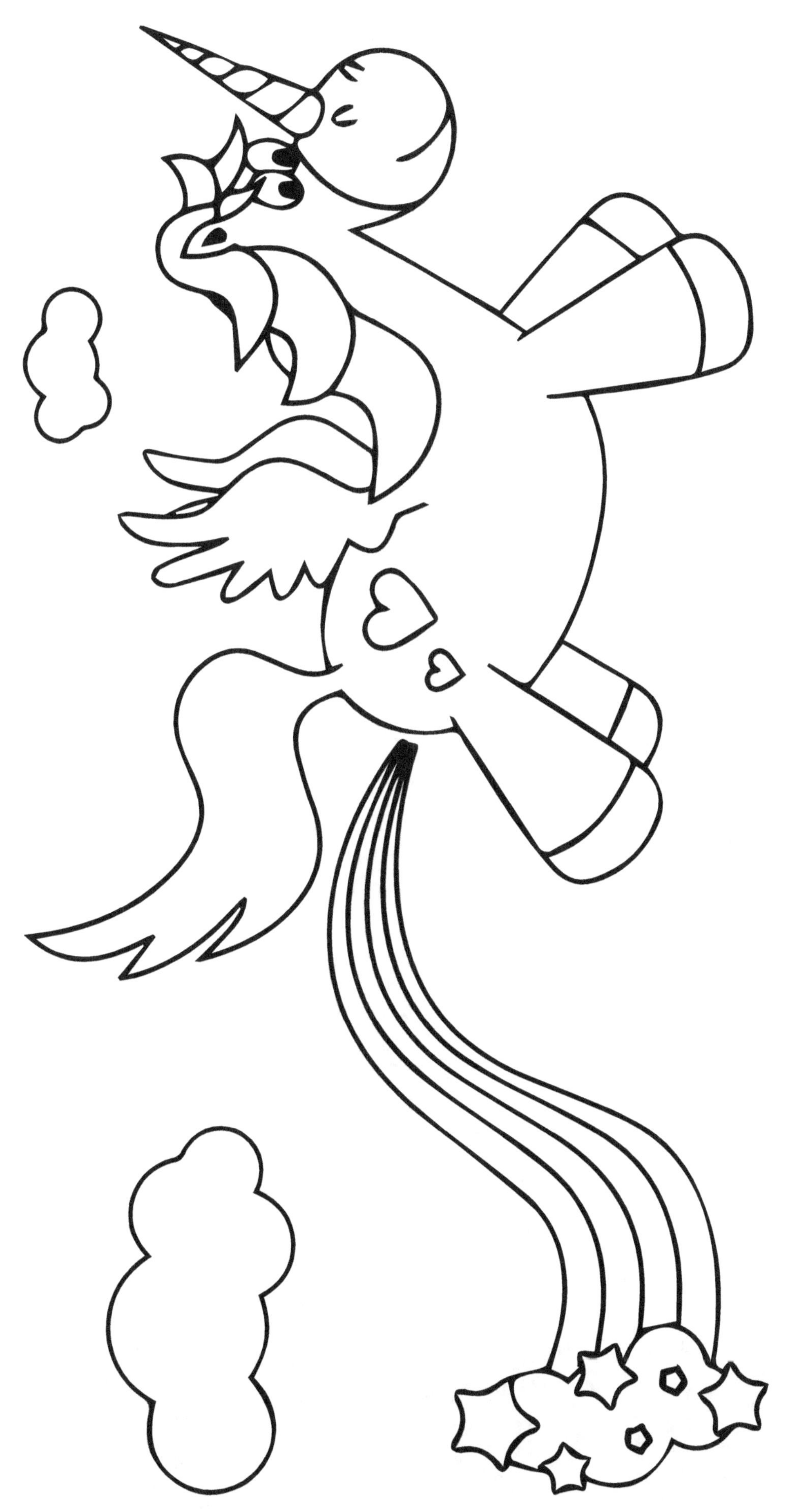

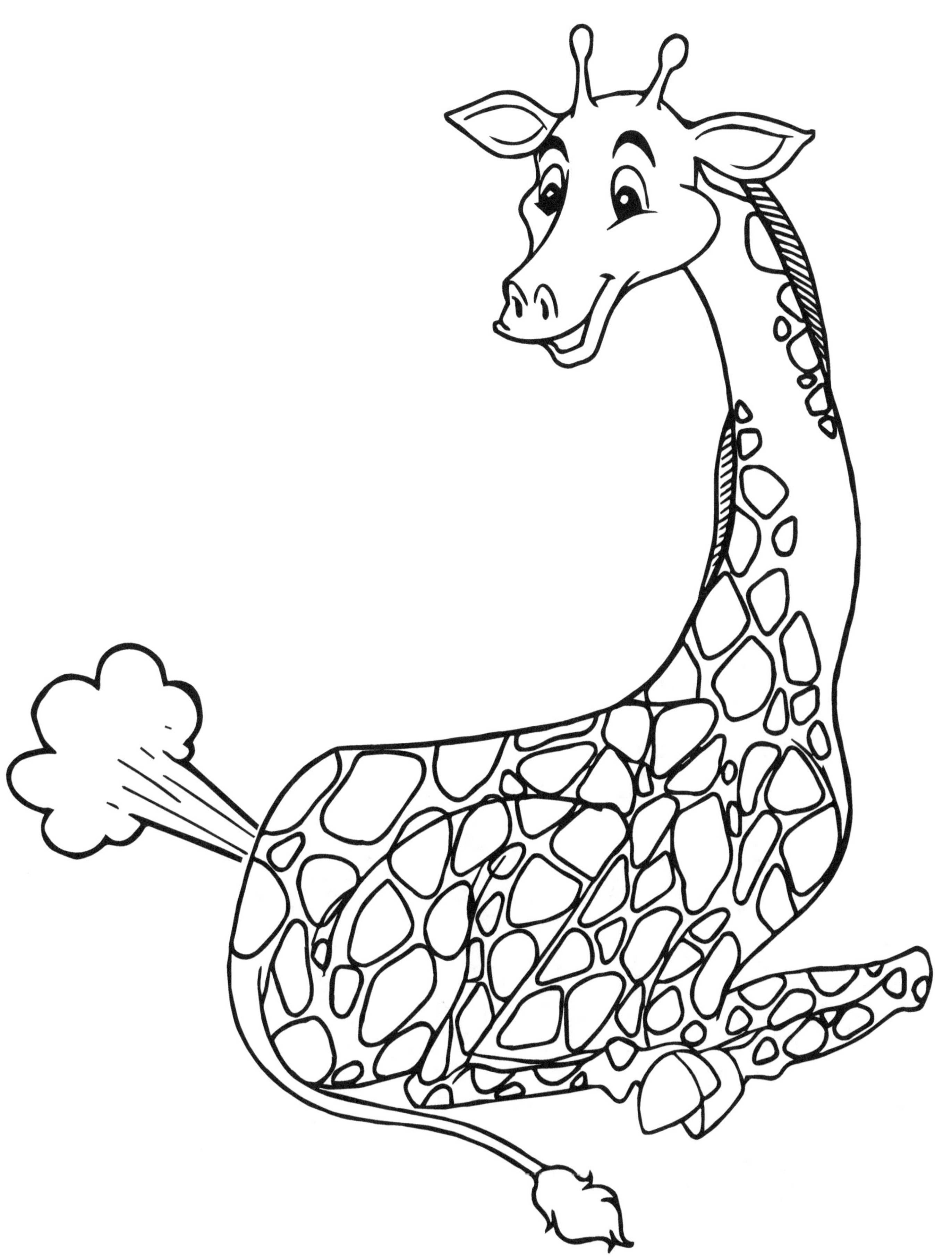

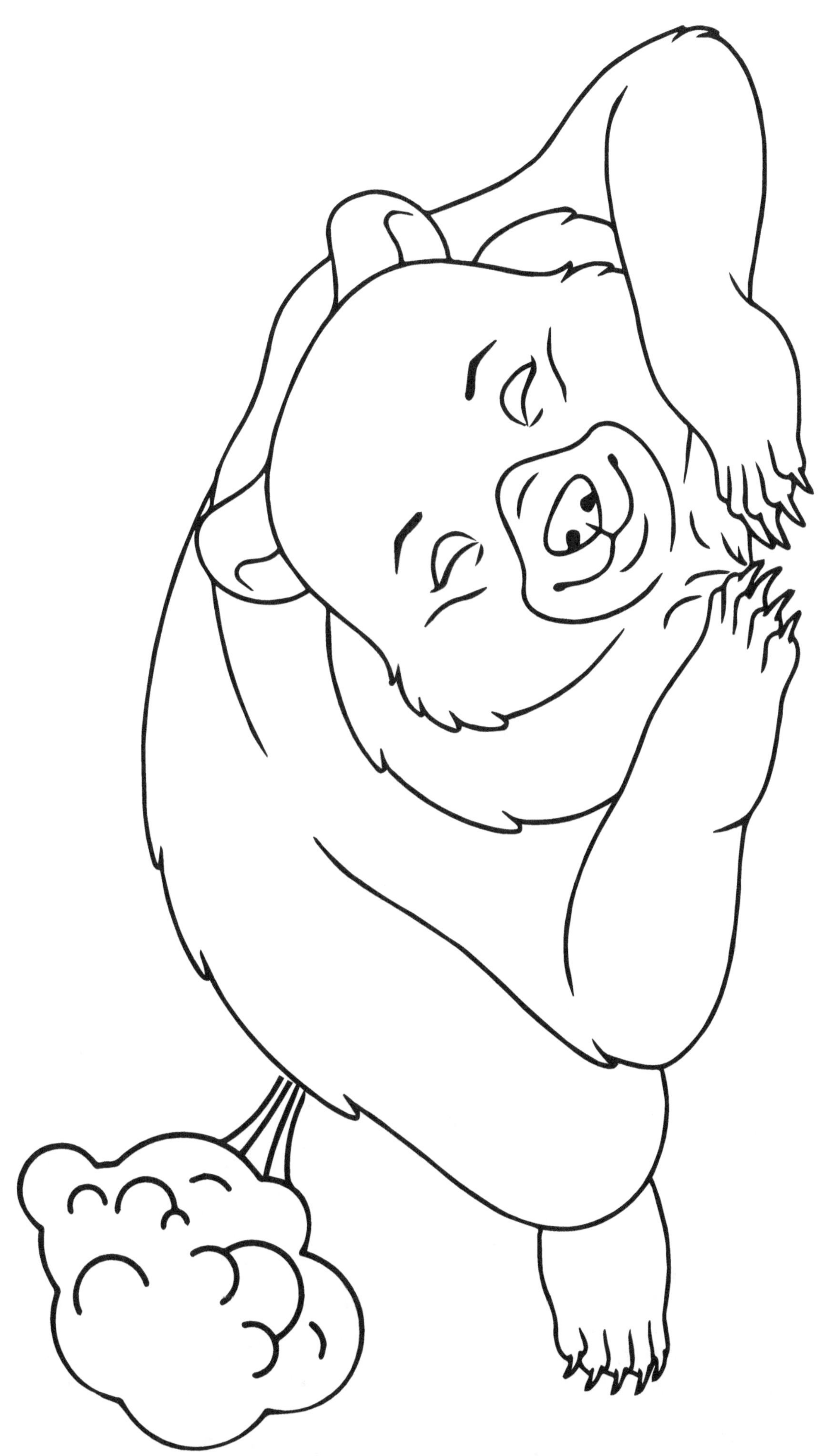

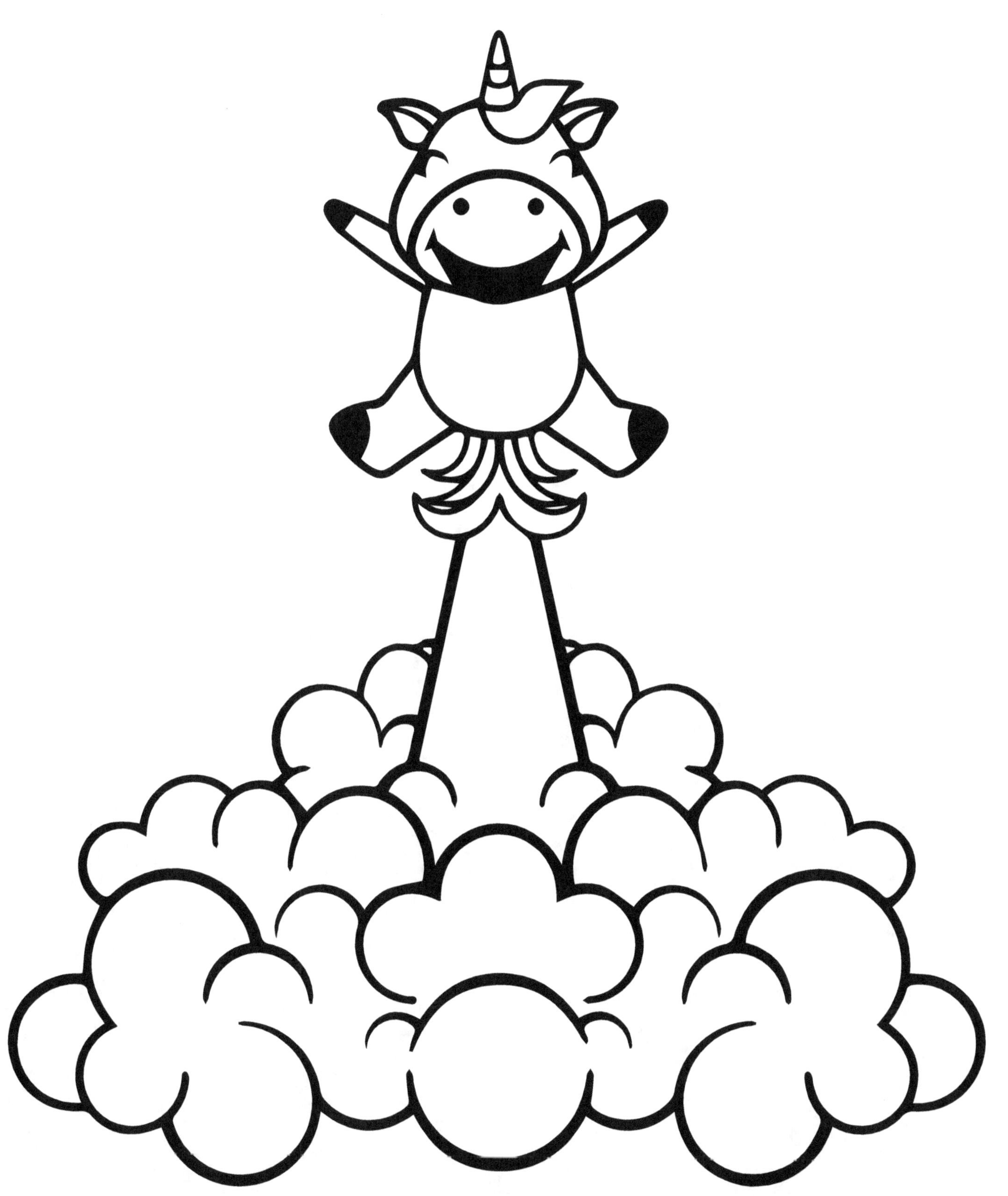

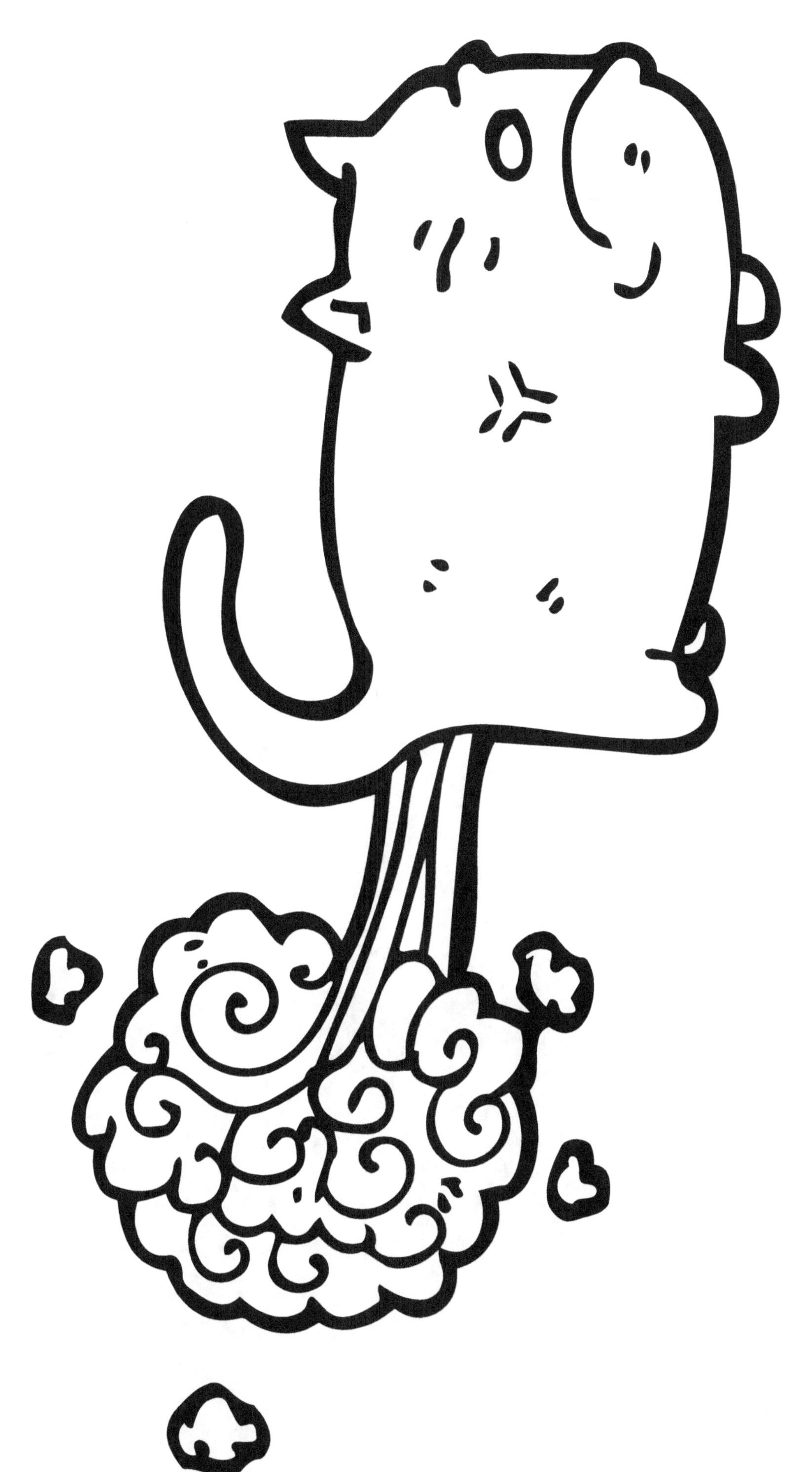

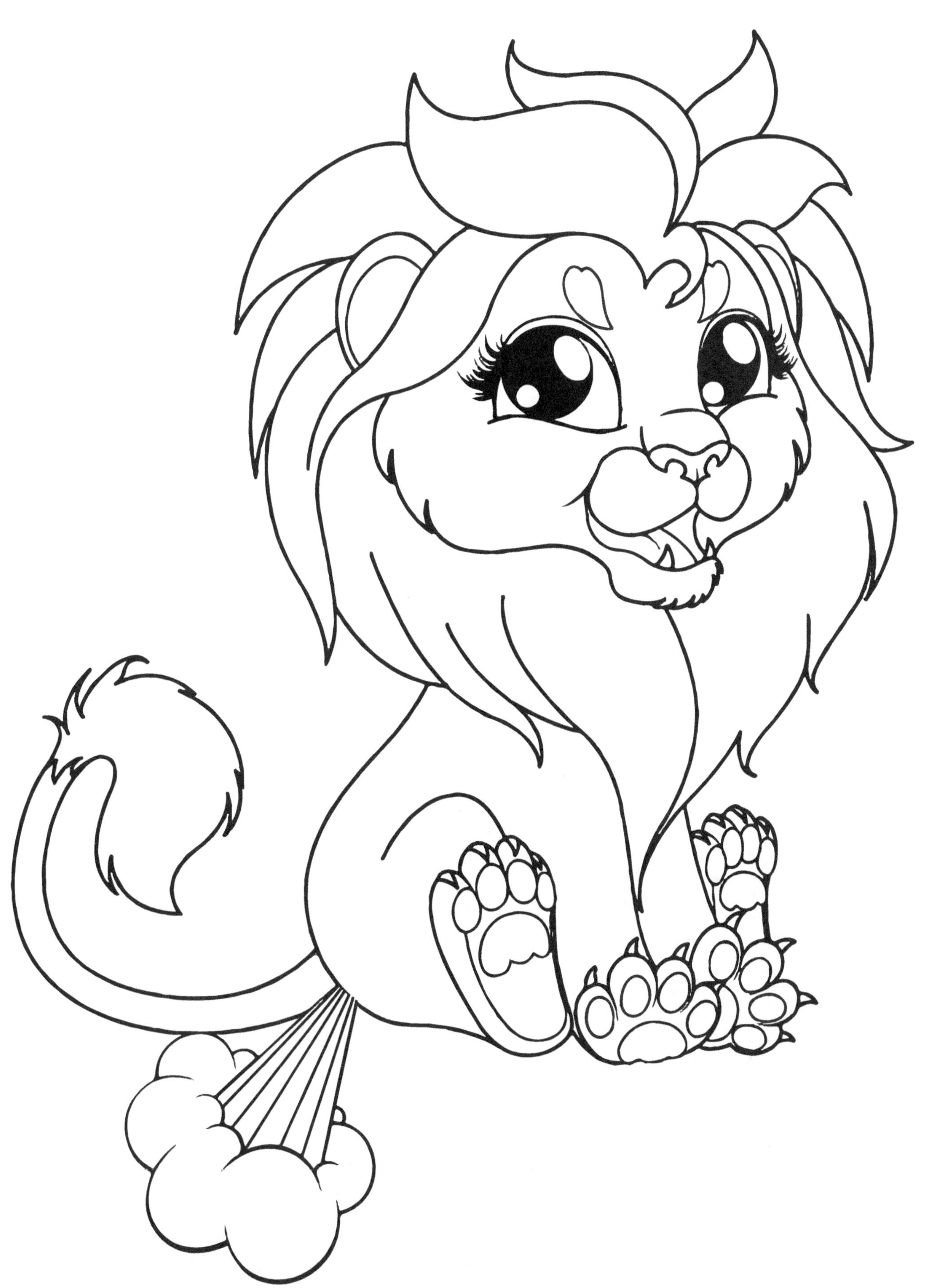

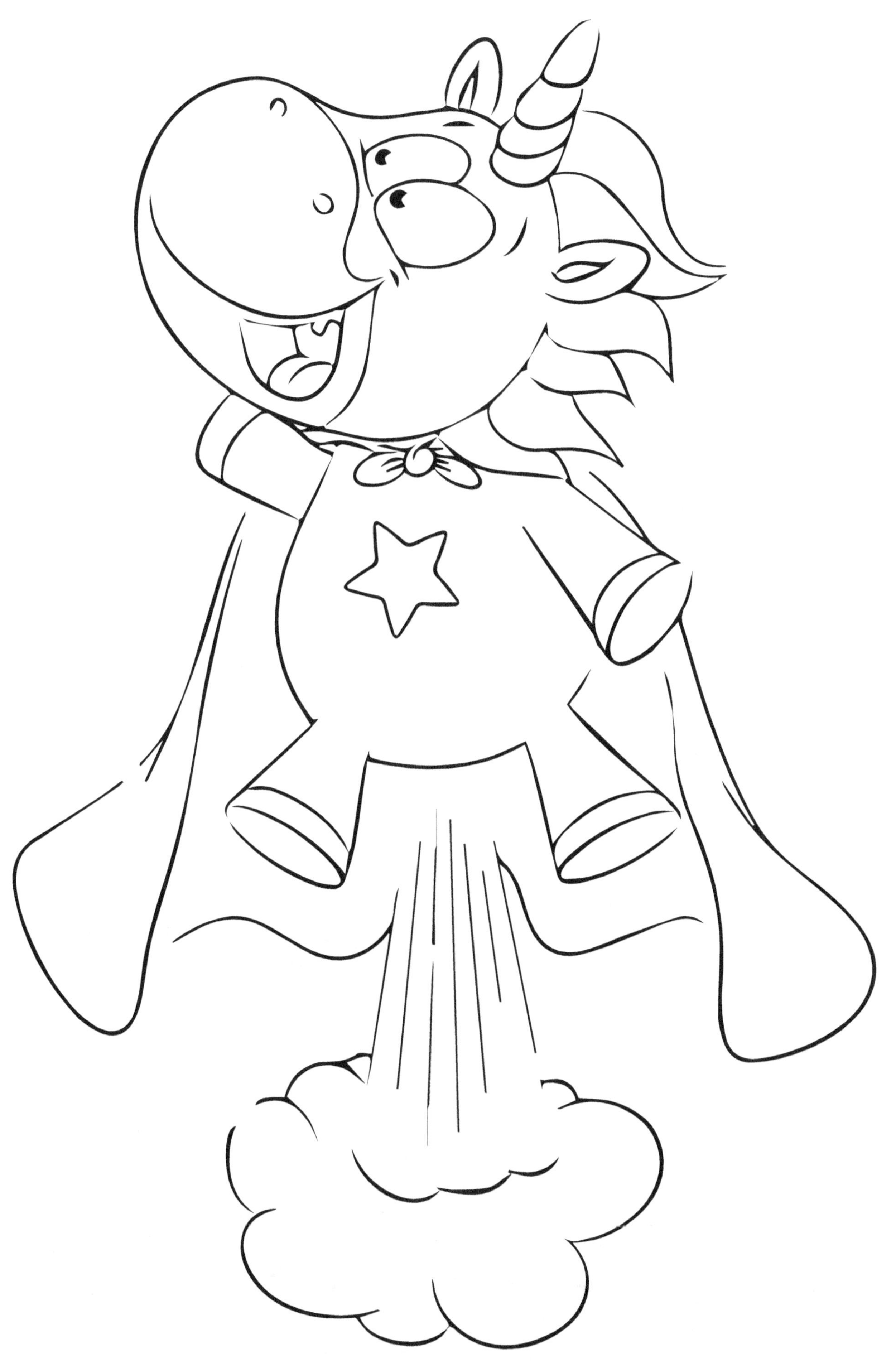

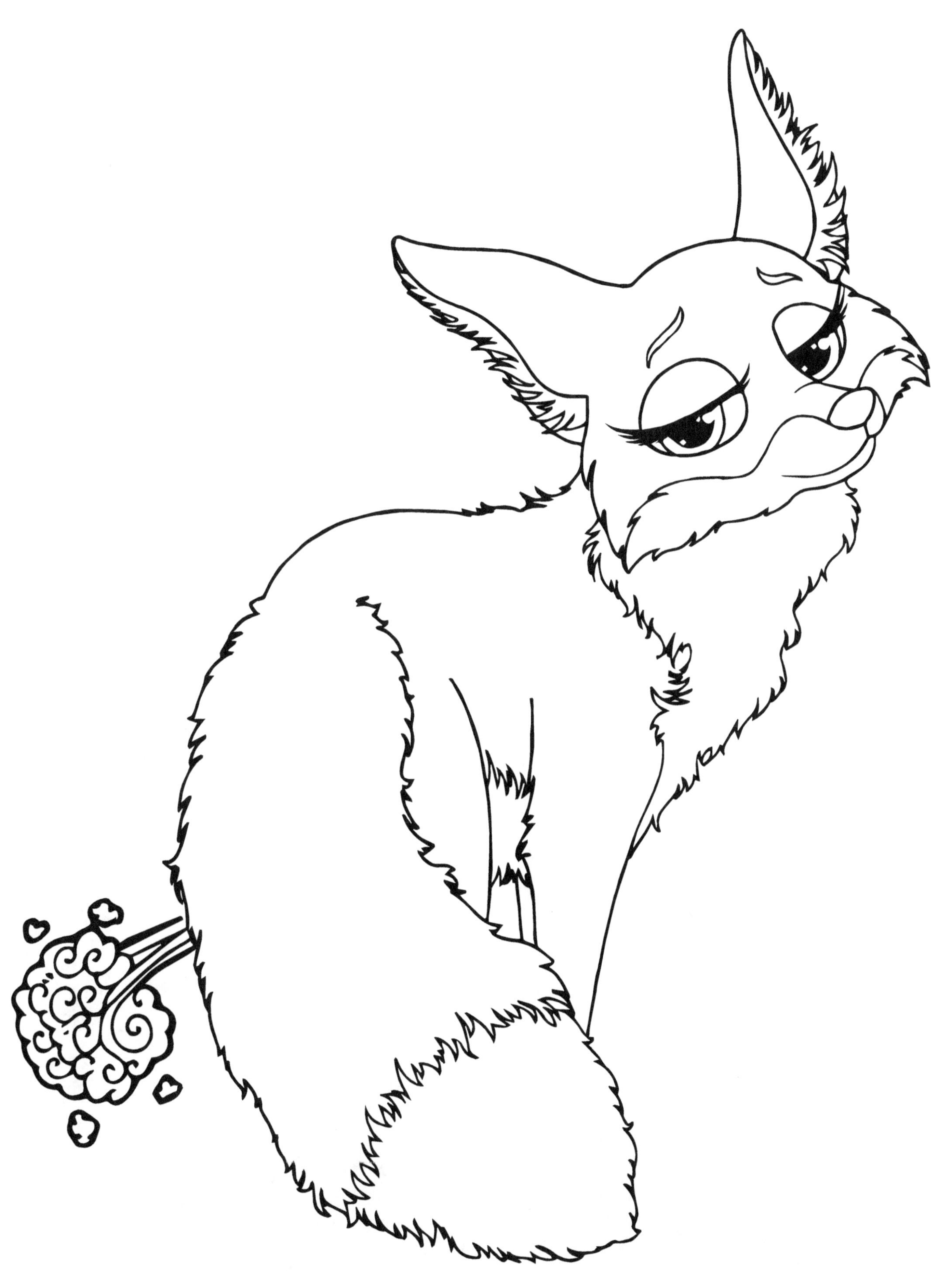

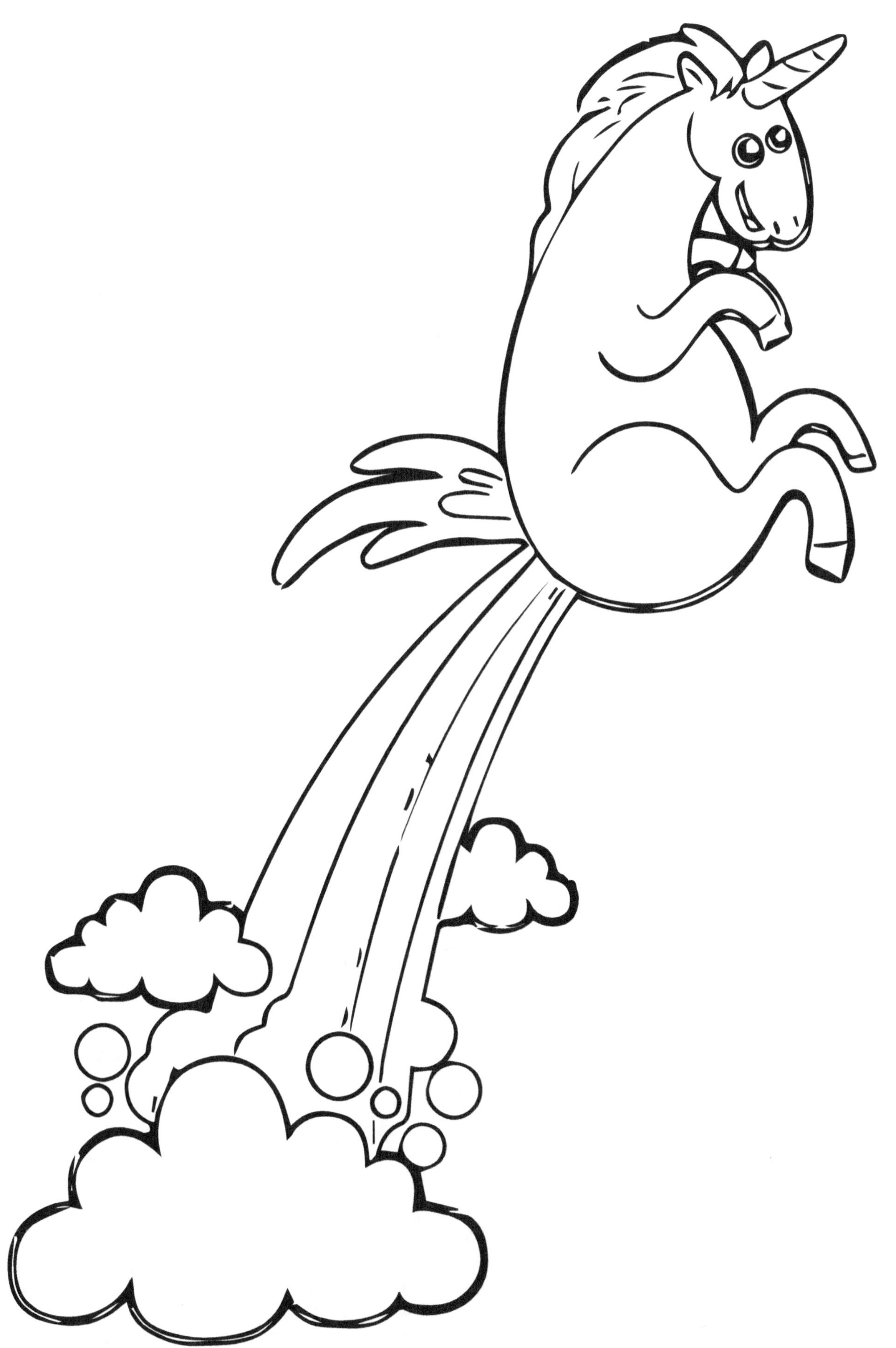

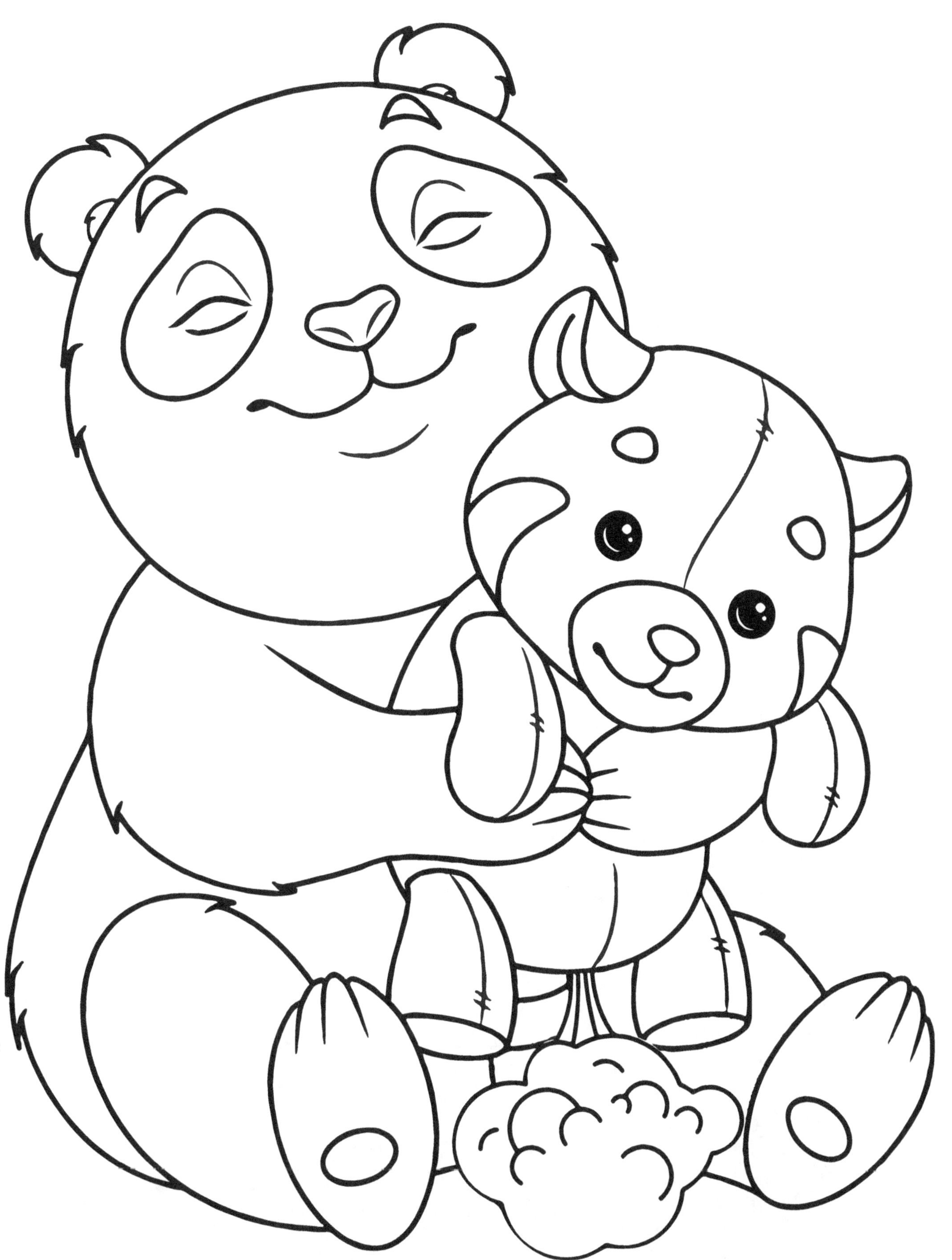

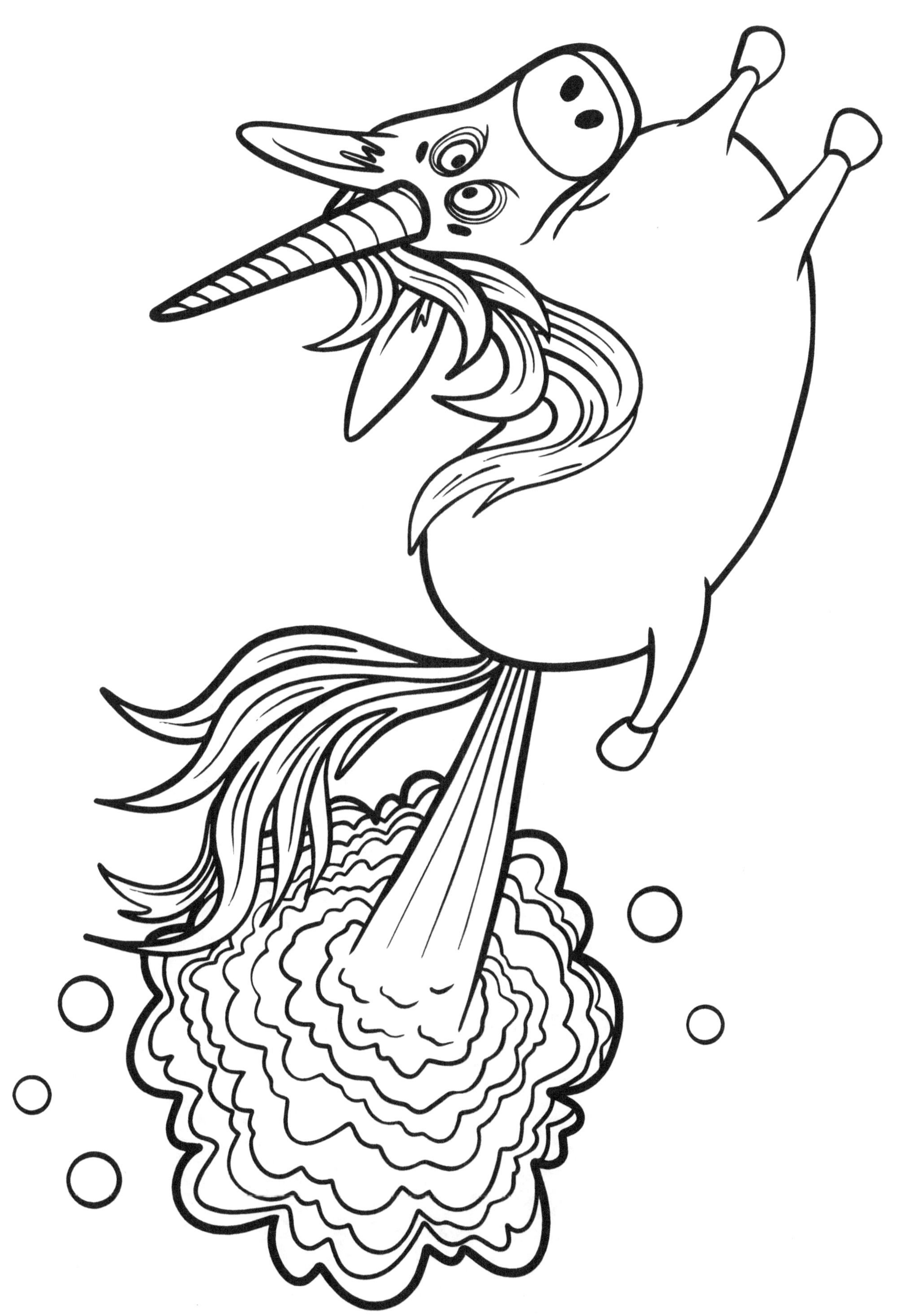

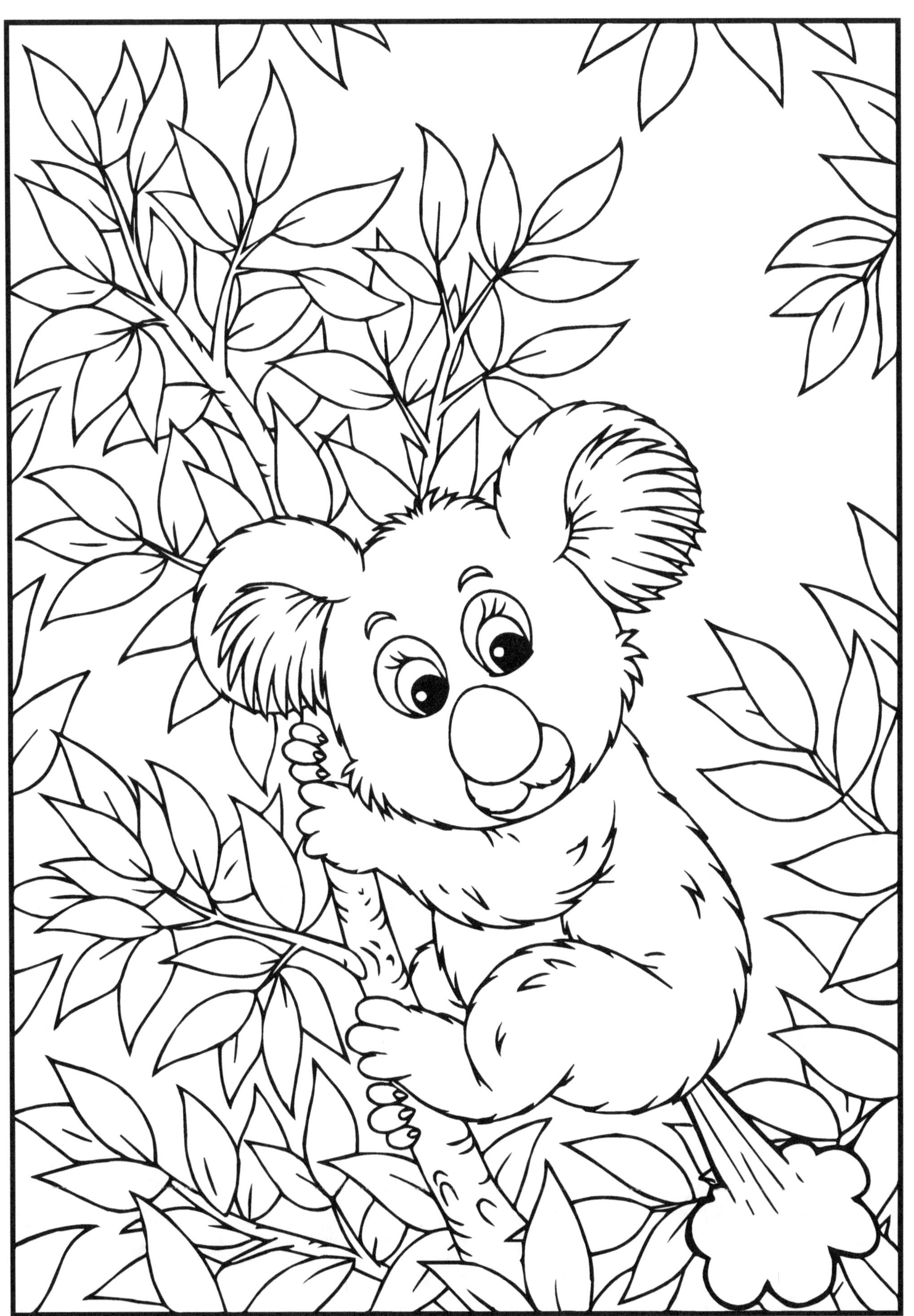

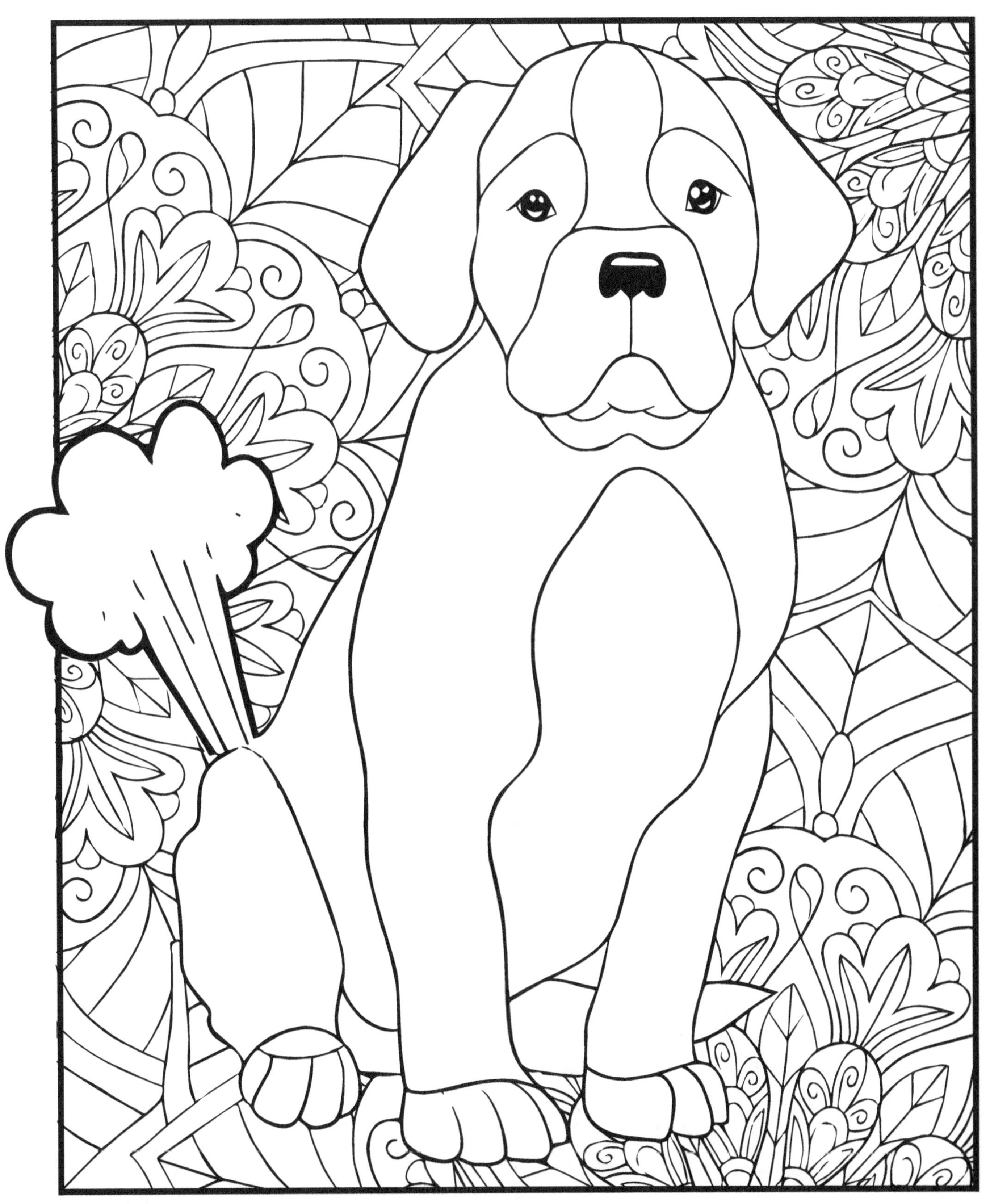